NON-MARKET COMPONENTS
OF
NATIONAL INCOME

Ismail Abdel-Hamid Sirageldin

SURVEY RESEARCH CENTER

 INSTITUTE FOR SOCIAL RESEARCH
THE UNIVERSITY OF MICHIGAN
ANN ARBOR, MICHIGAN

ACKNOWLEDGMENT

In addition to the many friends and colleagues at the Institute for Social Research and The University of Michigan who helped in many ways in the work that went into this report, the author wishes to express his special thanks to Professor James N. Morgan for suggesting the importance of this problem and for his guidance, valuable suggestions, and intellectual stimulation. Discussions with Professor W.H.L. Anderson helped clarify many otherwise ambiguous ideas and guided the research towards essentials.

The completion of this research would have been impossible without the cooperation of the staff of the Survey Research Center of The University of Michigan. I am deeply indebted to them for using their computing facilities.

Thanks are due to Mrs. Mildred Dennis for typing this report. Finally, the author wishes to acknowledge the constant encouragement and companionship of his wife whose home production proves the important economic role of non-market productive activities.

TABLE OF CONTENTS

                                                                    Page

ACKNOWLEDGMENT...   ii

LIST OF TABLES...   iv

LIST OF ILLUSTRATIONS..................................   ix

Chapter

1.   INTRODUCTION.......................................   1

2.   THEORETICAL AND CONCEPTUAL CONSIDERATIONS UNDERLYING...   5
      THE ANALYSIS

      2.0   Introduction..................................   5

      2.1   The Data Used in the Analysis.................   6

             2.1.1 The unit of analysis

             2.1.2 The sample used

      2.2   A Theoretical Framework.......................   7

             2.2.1 Analytical approaches to the valuation
                    of families' real incomes

             2.2.2 The value of time

             2.2.3 Classification of activities: the
                    scope of estimates

      2.3   Conceptual Difficulties.......................   20

             2.3.1 People in disequilibrium situations:
                    unemployed or sick for part of the
                    time or dissatisfied

             2.3.2 People with no reported hourly earnings

      2.4   Further Adjustments to Hourly Earnings........   31

             2.4.1 Marginal income taxes

             2.4.2 The journey to work

             2.4.3 Capital income

2.5   Problems Not Dealt With in the................... 38
       Analysis

2.6   The Procedure Used in the Analysis:............. 39
       A Summary

3.   EMPIRICAL CONSIDERATIONS UNDERLYING THE ANALYSIS........ 42

3.0   Introduction..................................... 42

3.1   The Sample Used.................................. 42

3.2   Sampling Variability............................. 43

3.3   Validity Of The Data............................. 46

3.4   A Note On The Tables............................. 52

4.   FAMILIES' FULL AND POTENTIAL INCOMES: 1964.............. 53

4.0   Introduction..................................... 53

4.1   Full Family Income............................... 56

       4.1.1 The determinants of full income

       4.1.2 The distribution of full income

       4.1.3 Full income among population groups

4.2   The Components of Non-market Income:............. 74
       The Effect of Methods of Valuation

       4.2.1 The value of housework and home
              production: opportunity costs versus
              real costs

       4.2.2 The value of volunteer work

       4.2.3 The value of time spent on education

       4.2.4 Income from car services and car
              consumption

4.3   Potential Income................................. 85

       4.3.1 The value of time lost because of
              unemployment or sickness

       4.3.2 The value of desired more or fewer
              hours of work

5.   FAMILIES' REAL WELFARE................................   95

     5.0   Introduction..................................   95

     5.1   Measures of Welfare...........................   96

              5.1.1 Adjustments for family needs

              5.1.2 Adjustment for leisure time

     5.2   The Distribution of Welfare in the U.S.A...... 104

     5.3   Families' Welfare Among Population Groups..... 108

6.   CONCLUSIONS... 120

BIBLIOGRAPHY.. 122

LIST OF TABLES

Table   Page

2-1   Average hourly earnings for various groups of............   9
      activities by states in 1964

2-2   Participation and disequilibrium in.....................   26
      the labor force, 1964

2-3   Adjusting hourly earnings for disequilibrium.............   27
      situations

2-4   Hourly earnings of heads of families in the labor........   30
      force, by education, age, sex, and race - 1964
      (in cents)

2-5   Hourly earnings of wives within age and.................   31
      educational groups

2-6   Marginal tax calculation, 1964..........................   33

2-7   Daily journey to work of heads of families and...........   36
      wives in 1964

2-8   Mean mixed labor capital income and the proportion.......   38
      of imputed income (return on real investment) within
      age of heads

2-9   Income adjustments......................................   41

3-1   Distribution of family income within family size.........   48
      (1964)

3-2   Weekly hours spent on regular housework.................   51

4-1   Means and medians of full and potential family...........   55
      income

4-2   Multivariate analysis of home mortgages.................   58

4-3   Whether have a mortgage by life cycle...................   58

4-4   Distribution, means, and medians of full and............   63
      disposable income, 1964

4-5   Full income, disposable income and housework,...........   65
      and disposable income by total income, 1964

4-6   Full and potential income by family size................   69

Table		Page
4-7	Full income and its component within age and............ educational groups, 1964	73
4-8	Mean difference between opportunity cost and........... market price estimate of the value of housework and home production within age and educational groups, 1964	76
4-9	The value of time devoted to education within........... age and educational groups, 1964	80
4-10	Car income within age and educational groups............	84
4-11	The gap between actual and potential income within...... age and educational groups	88
4-12	Value of unemployment or sickness by desire for......... more or fewer work	90
4-13	Average value of desired more or fewer hours............ within age and educational groups	93
4-14	Average value of desired more or fewer hours by......... occupation	94
5-1	Schedule of estimated annual costs of goods and......... services	98
5-2	EQV full income by the desire for more or less.......... work and EQV full income welfare measure	103
5-3	The distribution of welfare measure.....................	106
5-4	Welfare measure, EQV. full income, and leisure..........	107
5-5	Mean welfare measure, EQV. full income, and leisure..... ratio by age and education	109
5-6	Characteristics used to explain welfare family.......... measure in 1964	113
5-7	Welfare measure in 1964: deviations for number......... of people	114
5-8	Welfare measure in 1964: deviations for age and........ education	115
5-9	Welfare measure in 1964: deviation for use of.......... new products	116

Table		Page
5-10	Welfare measure in 1964: deviation for............... whether own a business	117
5-11	Welfare measure in 1964: deviation for............... occupation	118
5-12	Welfare measure in 1964: deviation for............... whether grew up on farm and present location	119

LIST OF ILLUSTRATIONS

Figure   Page

2-1   The allocation of time in the various activities........   23

2-2   Marginal tax rates by total income tax, 1964   34

4-1   Lorenz curve: full family income and disposable.........   62
       income, 1964

4-2   The ratio of non-market income and disposable...........   66
       income by total family money income

4-3   The ratio of non-market income to disposable............   68
       income by family size, 1964

4-4   Mean full and potential income by race..................   71

4-5   Mean difference between opportunity cost and............   75
       market price estimates of the value of housework and
       home production by full family income, 1964

4-6   Value of volunteer work by the log of disposable........   78
       income, 1964

4-7   Car income by disposable income.........................   83

4-8   The gap between actual and potential income within......   87
       occupational groups

5-1   Mean EQV. adult measure by number of people in..........   99
       family

5-2   Income, leisure, and welfare contours...................   101

5-3   The distribution of welfare among population groups.....   111

CHAPTER I

INTRODUCTION

Estimates of the United States National income published by the
Department of Commerce have at least the following deficiencies. The
first is that they do not include the value of unpaid productive
activities done by the family, such as the value of housework, of home
production (do-it-yourself), or the value of time spent by heads of
families and their wives on doing or receiving volunteer work or taking
further education. Many students of national income accounts argue
that the exclusion of the value of those non-market productive
activities might result in biased estimates of rates of growth of real
output and make comparisons of levels or changes in national incomes
among different countries unreliable.[1]

The second deficiency is that they exclude the service income
received from consumer durable goods with the exception of the house.
Also, no estimates are given for the income received by the families
from the services of public goods such as highway, parks, or public
libraries. Not all families have access to public facilities and the
quality of public services received varies from one family to the other.
Finally, an important deficiency of the official statistics is related

---

[1]As Kuznets put it "The exclusion of the products of the family
economy, characteristic of virtually all national income estimates,
seriously limits their validity as measures of all scarce and disposable
goods produced by the nation.", Simon Kuznets, National Income and Its
Composition, 1919-1938. (New York: National Bureau of Economic Research
1941), 10.

1

to the concept of national income as a measure of real welfare and its
distribution. Nowhere in the accounts could we assess the impact of
sickness, unemployment or dissatisfaction with hours of work on the
potential labor force participation or on the distribution of real
welfare either where people have unwanted leisure at a given time or
where there has been a voluntary shift in people's preferences between
work and leisure.

The first objective of this study is to estimate the value of
non market output, namely the value of those non-market activities
done by American families in 1964 which were not included in the
conventional national accounts, the value of car services as part of
family income, the value of labor time lost because of sickness or
unemployment, and the value of more or fewer desired hours of work
by working heads of families. No attempt, however, is made to estimate
the services of other consumer durables since we do not have adequate
information about their values. Such exclusion is partially remedied
to the extent that the acquisition of such durables is reflected in the
imputed rents of home owners. Also, no attempt will be made to estimate
the value of services received from public facilities.

Two sets of estimates based on the cost of time devoted to non-
market activities are given.[2] The first estimate is done by grouping

---

[2] In a recent study by the Survey Research Center of the University
of Michigan, the allocation of time between market and non-market productive activities, among other things, has been examined in detail. See
James N. Morgan, Ismail Sirageldin, and Nancy Baerwaldt, Productive
Americans, (Ann Arbor: Survey Research Center, Monograph 43, 1966).
In the present study, by using the same set of data, we attempt to
impute values for those time estimates and examine their effect on the
distribution of family incomes.

activities into relatively homogeneous groups, namely, regular housework, painting and repairs, sewing and mending, growing food, volunteer
work, education, and other unpaid productive activities. The time
spent on each of these activities is then valued at the average market
price of labor performing the same type of activity. The second
estimate of these non-market productive activities is based on the
assertion that time is a scarce resource. The opportunity cost of time
devoted to any activity is its foregone earnings if devoted to another
activity. A theoretical framework is developed to integrate the
productive and consumptive activities of the family and to determine
the distribution and relative price of time among the various activities.
It is postulated that people, in equilibrium, value their time in their
various activities at their marginal hourly earnings net of taxes. But
more than one third of the civilian labor force were not in equilibrium
during 1964 because of sickness, unemployment, or mere dissatisfaction
with the institutional constraints on their time allocation. Thus, a
scale is developed to adjust their reported hourly earnings before
using it to estimate the value of their time devoted to unpaid productive
activities. Also, a multivariate analysis is performed to predict and
assign hourly earnings for potential workers like housewives who were
not in the labor force in order to estimate the value of their unpaid
productive activities. The basic theoretical framework underlying
the analysis is discussed in Chapter 2.

The empirical results presented are obtained from analysis of
cross-section data collected in 1965 by the Survey Research Center of
the University of Michigan. Chapter 3 discusses the sample used and
problems of inference from a sample statistic to the whole population.

The second objective of this study is to discuss, in light of the findings, the distribution of family incomes and to develop various measures of families' real welfare. Distributions of the estimated components by various demographic characteristics are given in Chapter 4. A more realistic estimate of aggregate real output, actual and potential, is then calculated by adding these estimated components to the conventional national income estimates. An estimate of real output lost because of sickness and unemployment is also given in Chapter 4 and the distributions of aggregate real output by age, education, and family structure are studied. In chapter 5 a discussion of income inequality in light of the findings is given. Various welfare measures are then compared and the chapter concludes by calculating for each family a welfare measure, which takes into account both the families financial needs relative to its composition and the leisure time available for the family during 1964.[3] The welfare measure is then treated as a dependent variable in a multivariate analysis in an attempt to explain differences in families real welfare in the United States.

Finally, the implications of the findings to economic policy and theory are discussed in Chapter 6.

---

[3] As K. Boulding put it "Per capita income is not the only test of economic efficiency and a rise in per capita income achieved by undesirably hard work and sacrificed leisure might represent a worsening of economic welfare", in "Some Difficulties in the Concept of Economic Input", in Output, and Productivity Measurement. (Princeton: Princeton University Press, 1961), p. 334.

CHAPTER 2

THEORETICAL AND CONCEPTUAL CONSIDERATIONS
UNDERLYING THE ANALYSIS

2.0   Introduction

One basic goal of the study is to arrive at estimates of
families' total real income by estimating some components of real output
which are neglected in the conventional national income accounts.   In
this chapter we shall discuss our procedure of estimating the net values
of time spent by heads of families and their wives on the various
productive activities originating in the non-market sector of the economy,
namely, housework, home production, volunteer work, taking further education, and the journey to work.   These by far constitute the largest
part of income neglected in the official national income statistics.[1]
Our theoretical problem could then be defined as setting boundaries on
families' productive activities and imputing values for their net output.

Since different assumptions will certainly provide different
estimates, we need to specify clearly a workable model of human behavior
which, at least, sets maximum and minimum limits on our estimated values
of unpaid productive activities done by the family.   An extension of the

---

[1]
    Services of consumer durables and public facilities will be discussed
in Chapter 4. Due to obvious difficulties consumer surplus will be ignored
in our estimates and leisure will be taken as a residual in the analysis.

conventional theory of individual economic behavior is necessary to meet such objectives.[2]

2.1   The Data Used in the Analysis

2.1.1 The unit of analysis

In this study we take the individual family as our basic unit of analysis.[3] This is because a vast majority of people in the world live under such social organization and also it appears to be the most analytically useful unit for our purpose. Decisions of family heads reflect complex interactions within each family. However, we assume that there exists for each family as a whole, an aggregate decision function (based on allocative efficiency), which we take as given, and we assume that the observed behavior of the various family members is, in fact, the result of such decision process.[4]

---

[2] In his famous work Kuznets argues that "Whatever criteria of social productivity used in estimates of national income...they imply an underlying scheme of values or social philosophy. The part of wisdom is to make this scheme of values explicit and allow it to guide the procedure, also,"...it is difficult to realize the degree to which estimates of national income have been and must be affected by implicit or explicit value judgement". Kuznets, op.cit., p. 4-5.

[3] A family unit is defined as all persons living together in the same dwelling unit who are related to each other by blood, marriage, or adoption. A single person who is unrelated to the other occupants of the dwelling or who lives alone is a family unit by himself. This is the definition used by the Survey Research Center of the University of Michigan.

[4] For a review of family research, see J. Morgan, "A Review of Recent Research on Consumer Behavior", Consumer Behavior, ed. L. Clark, (New York: Harper & Bros., 1958) 92-219. See also his forthcoming "Economic Viewpoint on Family Research".

2.1.2 The sample used

Data obtained through personal interviews with 2214 adults, (representing 2214 families), during January and February 1965 are the basis for the analysis in this study. A full discussion of that Survey and an evaluation of the data are given in Chapter 3 below.

2.2   A Theoretical Framework

2.2.1 Analytical approaches to the valuation of families' real incomes

In general, there are two approaches to the valuation of families' real output: (1) the market cost approach, (2) the opportunity cost approach.[5] Both approaches are deficient in some way or another, but we are going to use both of them and compare the results.

(a)   Real costs

In using market costs we imply that families occasionally employ servants, domestic help, and other personal services for the home as such. Their wages and salaries are market prices and are usually listed along with interest paid to non-personal lenders. Accordingly, all that we need is to multiply the relevant average market wages for such services by the total hours reported doing that service.[6] The practical

---

[5] For a summary of literature see: Marie, G. Gage, "The Work Load and Its value for 50 Homemakers, Tompkins County, New York" (Unpublished,Ph.D. Dissertation, College of Home Economics, Cornell University, 1960).

[6] This is essentially Kuznets' procedure where he attempted to estimate the value of housewives' services at prices paid to domestic servants. However, he argued further, that "though the only practicable one, this solution overlooks an important element making for lack of comparability between non-market goods and seemingly identical market goods. The purchaser of the latter ordinarily has considerable freedom of choice and opportunity to change, for example, a household can choose many types of servant, hire on trial and dismiss as often as it is so inclined: a gentleman would not treat his wife so summarily". This indeed implies a special type of family decision functions (complete autocracy) which is not generally true, Kuznets' National Income, pp. 22- 419-435).

difficulties are those of definitions and the lack of reliable data on domestic help. The survey data did not readily give sufficiently detailed classifications and some editing and coding work had to be done with the original interviews. Unpaid productive activities have been classified into six major groups namely: (1) regular housework; (2) painting and repairs; (3) growing own food and canning and freezing; (4) sewing and mending; (5) taking further education; and (6) volunteer work. Table 2-1 gives the various prices employed in the analysis with their sources.

The value of an hour spent doing housework is estimated at $1.31, painting and repairs $2.44, sewing and mending $1.79, and of an hour spent growing food or canning and freezing at $1.08. A state index of wages of productive workers of manufacturing industries is used to deflate those hourly wages to account for between-state price differences. This state index varied from 69 percent for North Carolina to 125 percent for Nevada. Hours spent on taking further education or doing volunteer work will be valued at net hourly earnings (opportunity cost criterion). This is the case, since volunteer work, for example, was not classified by type in the survey, which leaves us with no basis to estimate market prices.

(b) Opportunity costs

The alternative approach, namely, that the opportunity cost of what is done at home equals the foregone earnings of the same labor input if offered on the market is equally appealing especially for its welfare implication. The theoretical basis for such calculations is developed

TABLE 2-1

AVERAGE HOURLY EARNINGS FOR VARIOUS GROUPS OF ACTIVITIES
BY STATES IN 1964

State	Productive Workers, Manufacturing Industries (a)	Regular Housework	Painting and Repairs	Sewing and Mending	Grow own Food and Canning and Freezing
	Index (percent)	Cents	Cents	Cents	Cents
U.S. Average[d]	100%	131[b]	244[c]	179[c]	108[c]
New England					
Maine	79	103	193	141	85
New Hampshire	79	103	193	141	85
Vermont	82	107	200	147	89
Massachusetts	94	123	230	168	101
Rhode Island	83	109	202	149	90
Connecticut	103	135	252	184	111
Middle Atlantic					
New York	103	135	252	184	111
New Jersey	105	138	256	188	113
Pennsylvania	101	132	246	181	109
East North Central					
Ohio	115	151	280	206	124
Indiana	111	146	271	199	120
Illinois	109	143	266	195	118
Michigan	123	161	300	220	133
Wisconsin	105	138	256	188	113

State	Productive Workers, Manufacturing Industries(a)	Regular Housework	Painting and Repairs	Sewing and Mending	Grow own Food and Canning and Freezing
West North Central					
Minnesota	104	136	254	186	112
Iowa	107	146	261	192	116
Missouri	100	131	244	179	108
N. Dakota	90	118	220	161	97
S. Dakota	93	122	226	166	100
Nebraska	93	122	226	166	100
Kansas	105	138	256	188	113
South Atlantic					
Delaware	105	138	256	188	113
Maryland	100	131	244	179	108
Dist. of Columbia	109	143	266	195	118
Virginia	81	106	197	145	88
N. Virginia	105	138	256	188	113
N. Carolina	69	90	168	123	75
S. Carolina	71	93	173	127	77
Georgia	76	100	185	136	82
Florida	83	109	204	149	90
East South Central					
Kentucky	91	119	222	163	98
Tennessee	80	105	195	143	86
Alabama	86	113	210	154	93
Mississippi	70	92	171	125	76

(continued Page 11)

State	Productive Workers, Manufacturing Industries(a)	Regular Housework	Painting and Repairs	Sewing and Mending	Grow own Food and Canning and Freezing
West South Central					
Arkansas	70	92	171	125	76
Louisiana	98	128	239	175	106
Oklahoma	93	122	227	166	100
Texas	96	126	234	172	104
Mountains					
Montana	107	140	261	192	116
Idaho	99	130	242	177	107
Wyoming	111	146	271	199	120
Colorado	108	142	264	193	117
New Mexico	91	119	222	163	98
Arizona	107	140	261	192	116
Utah	109	143	266	195	118
Nevada	125	164	305	224	135

(continued Page 12)

State	Productive Workers, Manufacturing Industries(a)	Regular Housework	Painting and Repairs	Sewing and Mending	Grow own Food and Canning and Freezing
Pacific					
Washington	118	155	288	212	128
Oregon	113	148	276	202	122
California	117	153	286	210	126

a
   Calculated from: U.S. Bureau of the Census Statistical Abstract of the United States: 1966 (Washington, D.C.: U.S. Government Printing Office 1966) Statistics by States, Table No. 335.

b
   Estimated from: U.S. Bureau of the Census Statistical Abstract of the United States: 1965 (Washington, D.C.: U.S. Government Printing Office 1965), p. 240-243. It is interesting to note that in a recent study by the Chase Manhattan Bank, it was reported that the average value per hour of housework activities weighted by the number of hours spent on the various activities was 143 cents which is a little higher than our national average ¢131.

c
   Calculated from: U.S. Department of Commerce, Office of Business Economics, Survey of Current Business: April 1966 (Washington: U.S. Government Printing Office), Vol. 46, No. 4, pp. 515,516.

d
   U.S. averages in the first row of the table are deflated by the calculated index of hourly earnings (by states) of productive workers for manufacturing industries as given in the first column.

in the next section. For those who are in equilibrium, the cost of one hour spent on unpaid activities is equal to the marginal wage rate, net of taxes. Disequilibrium situations will be discussed in the following sections.

2.2.2 The value of time[7]

We regard the family unit as a technical unit in which commodities are produced, sold, or purchased.[8] Its manager (or board of directors!) decides on the allocation and utilization of total input resources (including time in all its uses) into a large number of activities or production relations, in order to maximize the expected utility of a stream of consumption of some basic commodities (activities). The family produces these basic commodities by utilizing market goods and services, non-market goods and services, and their available time resources in a given period subject to some 'objective' technical production relations, and to the family's budget and time constraints.

The system can be summarized as follows:

(1) $U = U(Z_1, Z_2, \ldots, Z_n)$ where U is an ordinal utility function and is assumed to have the ordinary convexity properties of a standard utility function, and where Z_i is assumed to be a measurable commodity which gives rise to utility (consumptive activities). The Z's are produced by the family through the following production relations:

---

[7] The following discussion has benefited from recent contributions by G.S. Becker, "A Theory of the Allocation of Time", Economic Journal, LXXV (September, 1965) 493-517, and K.J. Lancaster, "A New Approach to Consumer Theory," The Journal of Political Economy, LXXIV (April, 1966).

[8] For a similar view which recognizes the household as a small factory, see A.K. Cairncross, "Economic Schizophrenia", Scottish Journal of Political Economy, (February, 1958).

(2) $Z_i = Z_i (\underline{X}_i, \underline{Y}_i, \underline{L}_i)$ (lines below letters indicate vectors)

where $\underline{X}_i = (x_{i1}, x_{i2}, \ldots, x_{ini}) =$ A vector of market goods and services used in producing Z_i (including a subset related to the flow of the services of capital goods),

$\underline{Y}_i = (y_{i1}, y_{i2}, \ldots, y_{i,si}) =$ a vector of non-market goods and services, used in producing Z_i,

$\underline{L}_i = (\ell_{i1}, \ell_{i2}, \ldots, \ell_{i,ci}) =$ a vector of time units used in producing Z_i (consumptive activities),

And where the partial derivatives of Z_i with respect to $\underline{X}_i$, $\underline{Y}_i$, and $\underline{L}_i$ are non-negative.

The family will maximize $U(\ )$ subject to a basic time constraint:

(3) $T = \underline{L} \cdot \underline{E}'_c + \underline{J} \cdot \underline{E}'_r + \underline{H} \cdot \underline{E}'_k$,   and to a budget constraint

(4) $\sum_i^n P_i X_i + \sum_i^s Q_i y_i = I = V + \underline{J} \underline{W}' + \underline{H} \underline{N}'$

where $P_i =$ The given market prices of goods and services bought by the family,

$Q_i =$ imputed prices of non-market goods and services used in producing Z's,

$V =$ non-earned income,

$I =$ total income,

$\underline{W} = (W_1, W_2, \ldots, W_r)$ = hourly earnings in the various occupations,

$\underline{J} = (j_i, j_2, \ldots, j_r)$ = hours spent in the various occupations,

$\underline{N} = (N_1, N_2, \ldots, N_k)$ = imputed \$/hr in the various non-market productive activities

$\underline{H} = (H_1, H_2, \ldots, H_k)$ = hours spent in the various non-market productive activities

$\underline{L} = (L_1, L_2, \ldots, L_1)$ = hours spent in the various consumptive activities (Z's), including leisure activities,

$E_m = (1, 1, \ldots, 1)$ = vector of unit elements.

The production relations (2), and the time and budget constraints (3) and (4) imply that given the flow of capital services, the family could either purchase no goods from the market (i.e., produce all its requirements of the Z's by its own effort, where $\underline{X}_i = \underline{0}$) or trade its own time for income by which it could buy goods and services.

In order to maximize (1) subject to (3) and (4), we form the following function:

$$(5) \quad U^* = U(Z_1, \ldots, Z_m) + \lambda_1 \left(\sum_{i=1}^{n} P_i X_i + \sum_{i=1}^{s} \left(Q_i Y_i \right) - V - \underline{J}.\underline{W}' - \underline{H}.\underline{N}' \right) + \lambda_2 (T - \underline{L}.\underline{E}'_c - \underline{J}.\underline{E}'_r - \underline{H}.\underline{E}'_k)$$

where λ_1 and λ_2 are Lagrangian multipliers. Taking the partial derivatives with respect to J_i, H_i, L_i, X_i, Y_i, λ_1, and λ_2 and setting them equal to zeros we obtain:

$$(6) \quad \frac{\partial U^*}{\partial J_i} = -\lambda_1 W_i - \lambda_2 = 0 \qquad i = 1, \ldots r$$

$$(7) \quad \frac{\partial U^*}{\partial H_i} = -\lambda_1 N_i - \lambda_2 = 0 \qquad i = 1, \ldots k$$

$$(8) \quad \frac{\partial U^*}{\partial L_{ij}} = -\lambda_2 + \frac{\partial U}{\partial L_{ij}} = 0 \qquad j = 1, \ldots l_i \; ; \; i = 1, \ldots m$$

$$(9) \quad \frac{\partial U^*}{\partial X_{ij}} = \lambda_1 P_{ij} + \frac{\partial U}{\partial X_{ij}} = 0 \qquad j = 1, \ldots n_i \; ; \; i = 1, \ldots m$$

(10) $\dfrac{\partial U^*}{\partial X_{ij}} = \lambda_1 P_{ij} + \dfrac{\partial U}{\partial Y_{ij}} = 0 \qquad j = 1, \ldots n_i \; ; \; i = 1, \ldots m$

(11) $\dfrac{\partial U^*}{\partial \lambda_1} = \sum_{i=1}^{n} P_i \, X'_i + \sum_{i=1}^{s} Q_i \, Y_i - V - \underline{J.W'} - \underline{H.N'} = 0$

(12) $\dfrac{\partial U^*}{\partial \lambda_2} = T - \underline{L.E'}_1 - \underline{J.E'}_r - \underline{H.E'}_k = 0$

where λ_1 can be identified as the marginal utility of money expenditure (from (9)), and λ_2 can be identified as the marginal utility of leisure (from (8)). In addition, we get from (6) and (7), and from (9) and

(13) $W = N = \lambda_2 \, / \, \lambda_1$, and

(14) $\dfrac{\partial U}{\partial X_{ij}} \div P_{ij} = \dfrac{\partial U}{\partial Y_{ij}} \div Q_{ij}$ [9/]

---

[9] An interesting implication of relation (14) is that the allocation of market and non-market goods and services in the production of the basic commodities (Z_i) are subject mainly to efficiency conditions (i.e., technical objective relations).

Thus, from (1) and (2) we have:

$$\frac{\partial U}{\partial X_{ij}} = \frac{\partial U}{\partial Z_j} \times \frac{\partial Z_i}{\partial X_{ij}} \qquad \text{and} \qquad \frac{\partial U}{\partial Y_{ij}} = \frac{\partial U}{\partial Z_i} \times \frac{\partial Z_i}{\partial Y_{ij}}$$

Substituting back in (14) we get:

$$\frac{\partial Z_i}{\partial X_{ij}} \div \frac{\partial Z_i}{\partial Y_{ij}} = \frac{Q_{ij}}{P_{ij}}$$

Under the assumptions of our model, the family will tend to allocate its time such as to make the value of its marginal product in its non-market productive activities (N_i's) equal to the marginal value product in its market activities (equals the marginal hourly earnings net of taxes), which are also set equal to the ratio of the marginal utilities of leisure and income, from (13). Otherwise, it will always pay to shift its resources between market activities, unpaid productive activities, and leisure or consumptive activities.

2.2.3 Classifications of activities: the scope of the estimates

The model developed in the last section implies that there are some activities H which are a perfect substitute for real output. This is indeed not universally true. Most productive activities yield both real output and utility or satisfaction. However, by concentrating on the opportunity cost of the use of time, we could group the various activities into those which have or do not have foregone costs in terms or earned income (i.e., by losing real output that would otherwise have been earned by working the same hours for money). If we assume that working for money yields only income but no satisfaction - a rather un-realistic assumption - then the opportunity costs (foregone earnings) of those activities which save money will be low, and will be lower the more the proportion of real output saved.[10] Voluntary leisure and other

---

[10] In a recent work, John Marsh and Frank Stafford demonstrated that academically employed professional and technical workers forego monetary returns relative to their private industry counterparts, using the hypothesis that attitudes toward work, namely professional and intellectual values, can be considered to measure compensation for monetary losses, "Income Foregone: The Effects of Values on Pecuniary Behavior" (National Opinion Research, University of Chicago, March 1966), (Mimeographed). The implication of such findings is that, in the case of professionals, reported hourly earnings is an underestimate of the marginal value product of their unpaid productive work.

consumptive activities, on the other hand, have very high opportunity

costs (foregone earnings). Thus, we define productive activities as those

which either make money or save money regardless of whether it was a

market or a non-market activity. However, we recognize that to the extent

that those activities produce satisfaction as well, we are underestimating

the total welfare of the family.[11]

For analytical purposes, productive activities will be classified

into work for money, journey to work, regular housework, home production

or do-it-yourself, education, and volunteer work activities.[12]

We notice, however, that our classification is not conclusive,

since we argue that in most cases the family members will be the best

judge on grouping their own activities as productive or non-productive.[13]

---

[11] A paint manufacturer advertised that his brand saves time and
will "turn you loose" from painting your own home (home production) to
play golf or to do other leisure activities. This might indicate that
recent developments in the American culture regard many housework and do-
it-yourself work as pure productive activities.

[12] Education is an investment activity. The individual will use his
time resource in education until the present value product of his time
invested, is equal to its present cost which is equal to his net hourly
earnings. See the discussion in Chapter 4.

[13] Nelson N. Foote, raised some analytical problem in "getting people
to make a record of their behavior" since there is usually a "low rate of
response and cooperation". He concludes that "Many of you may have tried
to get people to give estimates of how often they watch television, how
long they usually take for breakfast, etc. Generally speaking - "I will
say this in one simple phrase - forget it. These estimates of how much
time people spend are worthless" Nelson N. Foote, "The Time Dimension and
Consumer Behavior" in Joseph W. Neuman (ed.), On Knowing the Consumer,
(New York: John Wiley & Sons, 1966), p. 39. We argue that this is rather
a strong assertion, since it all depends on the question asked and the
details of time use required. These analytical points are discussed in
more detail in Chapter 3.

This is as it should be, since it is their own relative valuation of their unpaid output which matters in allocating their time after all. More important, estimates based on families' own distinction between consumption and productive activities will incorporate shifts in their preferences over time and thus makes temporal comparison of real income more meaningful. In other words, we define a family's total production to include its earned income and the value of all types of non-market activities which the family does either to make or save money, to increase its earning potential (e.g., investment in human capital), or to engage in other activities which are regarded productive from the society's point of view like volunteer work.

In conventional national income accounts, the value of output generated from work for money is computed as wages and salaries plus the imputed values of payment in kind to employees. Creation of income through home-grown food and home additions and repairs have been estimated by Morgan and others.[14] Their estimates, however, constitute but a small part of total families' direct production. Although there has been recently a wide discussion about the concept of human capital and its value, no estimates of its value added in a national income framework are available except as it is paid for in wages or money earnings. Finally, there are estimates of volunteer contributions but not of volunteer work although only the latter could be considered as net value to the society while the former is a transfer transaction which does not add to the flow of real goods and services.

---

[14] James Morgan, M. David, W. Cohen, and H. Brazer, Income and Welfare in the United States, (New York: McGraw Hill, 1962), pp 95-105.

It is evident from the previous discussion that the neglected components of families' output in the national income accounts are grouped under journey to work, regular housework, most of home production, adult education, and volunteer work.

2.3   Conceptual Difficulties

Our discussion of the opportunity cost approach thus far assumes that the value - to the family - of a unit of its time used at home instead of sold in the labor market equals its opportunity cost which is equal to the marginal real wage rate net of taxes. Thus given the families' time allocation, and their hourly earnings, we could calculate the value of their unpaid work (using their marginal hourly earnings net of taxes). This procedure, however, is applicable only for those who were in equilibrium: who were not sick or unemployed, or who did not want more or fewer hours of work. Furthermore our previous argument assumes that families have complete freedom to allocate their time between market and non-market activities. In other words, the use of hourly earnings - if available - is relevant only where time is optimally allocated - where people are in equilibrium. This is indeed not the case in practice, for the following reasons:

   (a) There are cases where people were sick or unemployed for
   a period of time which render any valuation of their unpaid
   productive activities based on their reported hourly earning
   unreliable

   (b) While it is true that there are people who are satisfied
   with their present allocation of their input factors among the
   various activities, there are many people among those who were

not sick or unemployed who would like to work more or less
hours for money than they are actually working (i.e., disequilibrium situations); and

(c) Cases where there are no reported hourly earnings such
as non-working wives, retired people, or those who did not
work at all during the period of the analysis for involuntary
reasons.

2.3.1 People in disequilibrium situations: unemployed or sick for part of the time, or dissatisfied.

For those who were working during 1964 but were sick or unemployed
for a part of the period or for those who were not satisfied with their
allocation of their productive use of time, the problem could be approached
through some simplifying assumptions. Assuming diminishing returns in
their unpaid production and consumption of leisure (diminishing marginal
utility), then hourly earnings for those who were unemployed or who
desired more hours of work are clearly an overestimate of the marginal
value of unpaid work. If we assume further that people, given the new
constraints on their working hours, will tend to equate the marginal
value product of unpaid work and the ratio of the marginal utilities of
leisure and income; then we could construct a scale which reduces reported
hourly earnings by the extent of sickness or unemployment.

The same argument, in reverse will show that reported hourly earnings would underestimate the marginal value of unpaid work for those who
desire to work less hours: if a man who feels overworked by job pressures
still does some work around the house he must regard its value rather
highly.

Figure 2-1 illustrates these situations. Time is measured on the horizontal axis where OO' equals the period of the analysis (i.e., total time available for the consuming unit). The diminishing marginal value product of unpaid production is given by the curve HH and the time spent on these activities is measured from right to left along O'O. The indifference map of the consuming unit between leisure and income is reduced to a single curve LL by assuming that the marginal utility of expenditure (MU_I) is constant for all levels of total income. This last assumption is needed to simplify the graphic presentation and is not essential to the main argument. Thus the LL curve represents a diminishing marginal utility of leisure. And the time spent on leisure and consumptive activities is measured from left to right along OO'.

For a given marginal wage rate OW_o (equals the average wage rate), the consuming unit will maximize his utility by allocating his time such that the marginal rate of substitution between income and leisure equals the marginal value product of unpaid productive activities which also equals the marginal wage rate net of taxes. OB hours of his time will be allocated to leisure and consumption, BC hours to work for money, and CO' hours to unpaid productive activities. The value of his earned income equals BB'C'C,[15] the value of his leisure equals the area under the LL curve to the left of BB',[16] and the value

---

[15]This estimate is possible from Figure 2-1 since we assumed that marginal hourly earnings are equal to the average.

[16]Notice that at some minimum hours OM (i.e., 8 hours per day) required for maintenance, the LL curve becomes vertical which indicates that for the consuming unit, the value of his life is very large.

FIGURE 2-1

THE ALLOCATION OF TIME IN THE VARIOUS ACTIVITIES

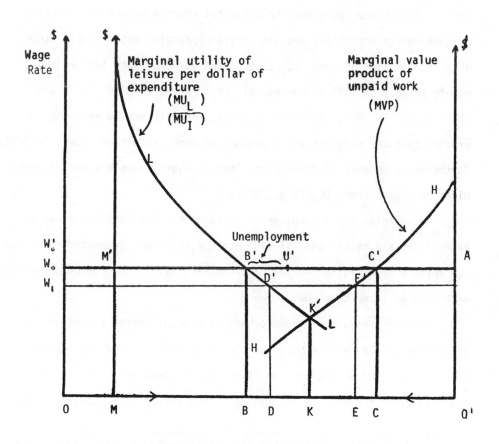

Time

of his unpaid productive activities equals the area under the HH curve
to the right of CC'. In actual calculations, however, surpluses are
ignored and our estimates (for equilibrium cases) will equal
(BB'C'C + CC' AO') for the value of paid and unpaid output and (MM'B'B)
for the value of leisure.

Now, let us assume that a family head was unemployed for BU'
hours. Then those hours must be allocated somehow between his leisure
or consumptive activities and his unpaid productive activities. Assuming
no shifts in the HH and LL curves, the value of both leisure and
unpaid production will be maximum at OW_1 (where D'E' = U'C' , and
DD' = EE'). Indeed at this new position, reported hourly earnings are
greater than the marginal value product of home production (i.e., $OW_o > OW_1$).
Furthermore, because of lower money income, hourly earnings net of taxes
might be higher than OW_o (e.g., OW_o').

If we relax the assumption of constant marginal utility of money
expenditure and assume that it did increase as income decreased, then the
LL curve will shift to the left and the marginal value product of unpaid
work will be lower than OW_1.[17]

An exact measure of unemployment or disequilibrium situations in
general must take into account the slopes of the LL and HH curves
and the extent of disequilibrium (i.e., an estimate of B'U'). Such
measures are not available in practice. The survey data, however, give

---

[17] It is also possible that because of sickness, for example, the
HH curve shifts to the left which reduces the marginal value product of
home production. The unlikely possibility, excluded from our consideration,
that both the LL and the HH curves shift upward to the point where
OW_1 is higher than OW (i.e., unemployed people will somehow become more
productive at their unpaid activities, or they will have an increasing
marginal utility of income).

us information about hours of sickness or unemployment by heads and wives
of families. It also gives us information about whether the head of the
family would like to work more or fewer hours (Table 2-2).

It was possible, by using the information of Table 2-2 to build
an index which approximates the extent of disequilibrium allocation of
time among the American people.

Table 2-3 shows our procedure of adjusting hourly earnings for
sickness, unemployment, or the desire for more or fewer hours of work.
The adjustment coefficients are assumed to be a simple function of the
extent of disequilibrium.[18] For example, if a person reports $3.00
hourly earnings net of taxes, was sick or unemployed for two weeks during
1964, and also desires more work, then we reduce his hourly earnings by
14.5 percent (i.e., 0.9 x 0.95) when valuing his unpaid work. With
reference to Figure 2-1, this means that OW_1 = .85 OW_o' where B'U =
two weeks of unemployment.

2.3.2 People with no reported hourly earnings in 1964: retired, housewives,
      or unemployed for the whole period.

For those who have a genuine choice but preferred not to work (e.g.,
housewives or retired people) or for those who wanted to work but had no
choice (e.g., the unemployed for the whole period) the cost of their
non-market activities could be considered as their foregone earnings.

---

[18] Essentially, we are faced with the familiar but basic problem
of converting qualitative responses into quantitative measures. We
chose a simple procedure, since sophisticated techniques do not claim to
reduce the arbitraryness in the choice of the conversion coefficients.
For a discussion of the analysis of qualitative material see, Dorwin P.
Cartwright, "Analysis of Qualitative Material", in Research Methods in
Behavioral Sciences, (New York: The Drydon Press Inc., 1953), pp 421-470.

TABLE 2-2

PARTICIPATION AND DISEQUILIBRIUM IN THE LABOR FORCE, 1964

I Heads of Families	Cases	Percent	Remarks
All cases	2214	100%	
Did not work in 1964	382	17	Hourly earning estimated and assigned Table 2-3,2-4
Worked in 1964	1832	83	
Not working in Jan-March 1965 (time of interviewing)	575	26	
Unemployed	94	4	
Retired	307	14	
Students	35	2	
Housewives	143	6	
Working in Jan-March 1965 (time of interviewing)	1639	74	Adjustments for disequilibrium Table 2-3
Like to work much more	83	4	
Like to work more	488	22	
Satisfied	849	38	
Like to work less	200	9	
Like to work much less	10	1	
II Housewives	1636	100%	
Did not work in 1964	889	54	Hourly earning estimated and assigned Table 2-5
Worked in 1964	747	46	

TABLE 2-3

ADJUSTING HOURLY EARNINGS FOR DISEQUILIBRIUM SITUATIONS

Cause of Disequilibrium	Heads of Families		Wives of Heads of Families		Multiply Hourly Earnings by
	Cases	Percent	Cases	Percent	
I. Sickness or Unemployment					
Worked in 1964					
Not sick or unemployed	1339	60	558	34	1.00
Sick or unemployed for 1 week	87	4	59	4	.95
Sick or unemployed for 2 weeks	558	3	22	2	.90
Sick or unemployed for 3 weeks	38	2	7	0	.85
Sick or unemployed for 4 weeks	45	2	15	1	.80
Sick or unemployed for 5 or more weeks	265	12	86	5	.75
Did not work in 1964	382	17	889	54	.70
All Cases	2214	100	1636	100	
II. Desire More or Less Work[a]					
Not in labor force	575	26			.90[b]
Desire (Much more) work	83	4			.90
Desire (More) work	488	22			.95
Satisfied	849	38			1.00
Desire (Less) work	200	9			1.05
Desire (Much Less) work	10	1			1.10

[a] The question was not asked for wives of heads of families

[b] These factors are applied to hourly earnings after being already adjusted for sickness and unemployment (i.e., multiplied by the factors in I).

In early 1965, when heads of families were asked about their employment status, 26 percent reported that they were not working as follows: 14 percent retired; 6 percent housewives; 4 percent unemployed; and 2 percent students. However, about one third of those 26 percent who were not in the labor force in early 1965 did some work for money during 1964 and reported hourly earnings. And the problem becomes that of estimating expected hourly earnings for the 17 percent of family heads and for the 54 percent of wives who did not work in 1964.[19]

Two multivariate analyses were made, a) to predict hourly earnings of heads of families, and b) to predict hourly earnings of working wives.[20]

(a)   Estimating hourly earnings for heads of families who did not work in 1964

A multivariate analysis of hourly earnings for heads of families who worked in 1964 showed that education, age, sex, and race are the most important factors in explaining differences in hourly earnings among family heads who were working.[21] It appeared that whether people have

---

[19] Those estimated and assigned hourly earnings, for the unemployed during the full year of 1964, will be reduced by 30 percent before using them to estimate the value of their unpaid productive activities since they were clearly in disequilibrium situations (see Table 2-3). The reason for this reduction could be readily visualized from Figure 2-1, where KK' becomes the lower bound for W_1.

[20] Our estimates are related to the individual's own perception of his expected earnings if he offered his services in the market but without actually doing that in practice. The underlying assumption is that his perceived hourly earnings are identical to the average hourly earnings of other earners having the same sex, race, age, and education.

[21] We used a newly developed multivariate analysis technique which divides the sample sequentially according to the most powerful discriminant variable over the whole sample and then over each relevant subsample. See John Sonquist, and James Morgan, The Detection of Interaction Effects, (Ann Arbor: Survey Research Center, Monograph No. 35, 1964).

college degrees accounted for the most significant difference in hourly earnings. We also found that age, sex, and race had different effects on the hourly earnings of those who have and those who do not have college degrees. For example, a white man without a college degree would be expected to earn 50 percent more on the average than a non-white man without a college degree but only 25 percent more if they had college degrees.

The procedure of assigning hourly earnings for family heads who did not work in 1964 is illustrated in Table 2-4. If an individual has between 6 and 8 grades of education, between 35 and 44 years of age, and is a white female, then her assigned hourly earnings = $1.98.

(b)   Estimating hourly earnings for non-working wives

A multivariate analysis of the hourly earnings of working wives showed that the age of wife and her education were the most important variables in explaining differences in hourly earnings of wives who worked in 1964. Table 2-5 shows the results of the analysis. Given Table 2-4 and 2-5 we assigned for all heads of families or wives who did not work in 1964 their predicted earnings had they offered their services in the market. Thus for a thirty year old housewife her predicted earnings will be two dollars per hour with a high school education and $1.25 without high school education.

TABLE 2-4

HOURLY EARNINGS OF HEADS OF FAMILIES IN THE LABOR FORCE,
BY EDUCATION, AGE, SEX, AND RACE - 1964
(in cents)

Age	(1) 18-24 yrs.			(2) 25-34 yrs.			(3) 35-44 yrs.		
Sex	Male		Female	Male		Female	Male		Female
Race Education	W[a]	N[b]	W	N	W	N	W	N	W	N
1. 0 - 5 grades	168	112[c]	90	203	135	108	232	154	123
2. 6 - 8 grades	216	144	115	261	174	138	298	198	159
3. 9 - 11 grades	255	170	136	308	205	164	351	234	187
4. High school	272	181	145	328	219	175	374	249	199
5. High school and training	281	187	150	339	226	181	387	258	206
6. College but no degree	313	209	167	378	252	202	431	287	230
7. College degree	358	287	255	409	328	291	558	447	397
8. Advanced degree	453	363	322	518	415	368	705	566	502

	(4) 45-54 yrs.			(5) 65 or older		
	Male		Female	Male		Female
	W	N	W	N	W	N	W	N
1. 0 - 5 grades	240	160	128	221	147	118
2. 6 - 8 grades	309	205	165	284	189	151
3. 9 - 11 grades	364	243	194	335	223	178
4. High school	388	259	207	356	238	190
5. High school and training	401	268	214	368	246	197
6. College but no degree	447	298	239	411	274	219
7. College degree	548	439	390	609	488	433
8. Advanced degree	692	555	493	770	617	548

[a]White [b]Negro [c]Estimated hourly earnings of Negro men and white women are put in the same column since there is no significant difference between them.

TABLE 2-5

HOURLY EARNINGS OF WIVES WITHIN AGE AND EDUCATIONAL GROUPS

Education	Less than 12 Grades			12 Grades but no College			College Degree		
Age	¢/hr(Std.Err.)		N	¢/hr(Std.Err.)		N	¢/hr(Std.Err.)		N
18-24	114	10	22	148	8	77	312	32	3
25-34	125	14	44	200	15	80	287	27	16
35-44	142	14	77	199	9	121	291	32	20
45-54	167	14	76	166	10	85	350	35	20
55-64	155	18	37	196	32	32	270	30	10
65+	114	51	11	148	58	2	250	66	4

2.4   Further Adjustments to Hourly Earnings

Our main objective thus far is to get an adequate measure of the value the individual places on his hours of unpaid work. Our theoretical development of the opportunity cost approach led us to use hourly earnings as a basis for that measure. In using that measure, however, we are assuming that reported average hourly earnings could be used as an approximation for marginal hourly earnings.[22]

---

[22] This might be a realistic assumption except for people with second jobs (15 percent of the labor force in 1964) or with overtime hours of work. No adjustments were made, however, since we have no information on individual basis, about second jobs or overtime pay.

In the previous section, we adjusted those reported (or assigned) hourly earnings for sickness, unemployment or the individual's dissatisfaction with the allocation of his time. In this section, we shall discuss three further adjustments, namely, adjustments for marginal Federal income taxes, for the journey to work, and for capital income.

2.4.1   Marginal income taxes

It is a common assertion in economic theory that the individual decides on the allocation of his time between work and leisure activities by reacting to his net rather than his gross wage rate (net of taxes).[23] Accordingly, we calculate, for each member of the family, his marginal hourly earnings net of taxes by multiplying one minus the marginal tax rate with respect to total family income by his reported hourly earnings. The marginal tax rate depends both on the size and structure of the family and on the level and sources of its income. Total taxes had been approximated in the Survey and are superior to the use of total family income for the purpose of our analysis, since they are already adjusted for exemptions, and since there is a simple systematic relation between taxes paid and the marginal tax rate. Table 2-6 and Figure 2-2 show the relationship between marginal taxes and total taxes paid for married couples (joint returns), heads of households (single heads but more than one-person families), and one-person families. For example, using Table 2-6, if the family paid $1-160 in total taxes, then their marginal tax rates in 1964, is equal to 16% and we multiply their reported hourly earnings by .84 to get their hourly earnings net of taxes which is then used to estimate the value of their time devoted to unpaid productive activities.

---

[23] See for example, Richard A. Musgrave, The Theory of Public Finance, (New York: McGraw Hill, 1959), 232-256.

TABLE 2-6

MARGINAL TAX CALCULATION 1964[a]

Joint Returns (married couples)		Heads of Households (single; more than 1 person)		Single People (1 person families)	
Total Tax	Marginal tax rate	Total Tax	Marginal tax rate	Total Tax	Marginal tax rate
0	00	0	00	0	00
1- 160	.16	1- 160	.16	1- 80	.16
161- 325	.165	161- 335	.17	81- 163	.165
326- 500	.175	336- 715	.19	164- 251	.175
501- 680	.18	716- 1155	.22	252- 340	.18
681- 1480	.20	1156- 1615	.83	341- 740	.20
1481- 2420	.235	1616- 2155	.27	741- 1210	.235
2421- 3500	.270	2156- 2735	.29	1211- 1750	.27
3501- 4720	.305	2736- 3375	.32	1751- 2360	.305
4721- 6080	.34	3376- 4055	.34	2361- 3040	.34
6081- 7580	.375	4056- 4805	.37	3041- 3790	.375
7581- 9220	.41	4806- 5585	.39	3791- 4610	.41
9221- 11000	.445	5586- 6435	.42	4611- 5500	.445
11001- 12900	.475	6436- 7305	.43	5501- 6450	.475
12901- 14920	.505	7306- 8215	.45	6451- 7460	.505
14921- 19200	.535	8216- 9155	.47	7461- 9600	.535
19201- 25920	.56	9156-11095	.48	9601- 12960	.560
25921- 32940	.585	11096-13156	.51	12961- 16470	.585
32941- 40260	.61	13157-14215	.53	16471- 20130	.610
40261- 47880	.635	14216-15295	.54	20131- 23940	.635
47881- 61080	.64	15296-17535	.56	23941- 30540	.66
61081- 74780	.685	17536-21045	.585	30541- 37390	.685
74781- 88980	.71	21046-22235	.595	37391- 44490	.71
88981-103680	.735	22236-27115	.610	44491- 51840	.735
103681-118680	.75	27116-29595	.62	51841- 59340	.75
118681-271680	.775	29596-33405	.635	59341-135840	.765
271681-and more	.77	33406-37305	.65	135841 or more	.77

[a] Calculated from J.K. Lassers, Your Income Tax, (New York: Simon and Schuster, 1965) Tables P21.00 - PP. 160-164.

FIGURE 2-2

MARGINAL TAX RATES BY TOTAL INCOME TAX (1964)

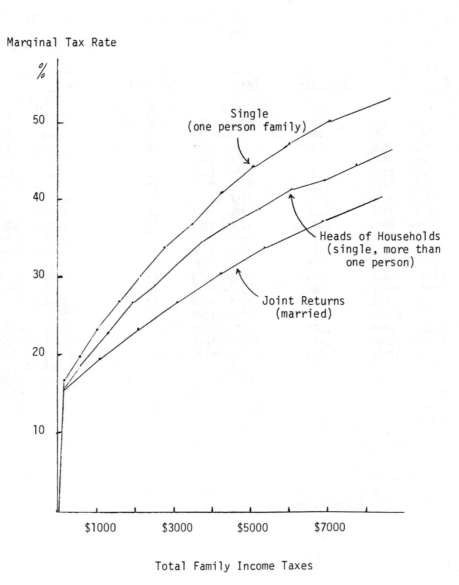

Marginal Tax Rate

Total Family Income Taxes

2.4.2   The journey to work

Hourly earnings are usually calculated, for each individual,
by dividing his total earned income by his total hours spent on the job.
This procedure assumes that the time spent on the journey to work is a
pure leisure or consumptive activity. This is not necessarily true.
On the other extreme, we could argue that the journey to work is a pure
work activity (i.e., in order for people to earn their income they must
go to their work places) and that hourly earnings have to be computed
by including the time spent commuting to and from work.

Whichever measure of hourly earnings will be used will affect
the imputed values of unpaid work and accordingly the measure of income
inequality. The distributions of hours spent on the journey to work
by heads of families and wives in 1964 are given in Table 2-7. However,
given the information at hand, it is impossible to calculate an adequate
measure of the leisure or consumptive component of the hours spent on
the journey to work (e.g., the difference between actual hours and
minimum hours required to go to work). Our analysis will be carried
out assuming that the journey to work is a pure work activity. Thus
hourly earnings will be calculated by dividing total wage income by the
sum of hours spent on the job and the hours spent commuting to work.

TABLE 2-7

DAILY JOURNEY TO WORK OF HEADS OF FAMILIES AND WIVES IN 1964[a]

(For 1639 heads of families and 747 wives working
for money in early 1965)

Daily Journey to Work	Heads of Families	Wives
None (lives where works)	9	9
1 - 22 minutes	24	35
23 - 38 minutes	19	17
39 - 52 minutes	11	12
53 - 75 minutes	20	15
76 - 119 minutes	6	5
120 minutes	8	4
Not ascertained	3	3
Total	100	100
Number of cases	1639	747

[a] Source: James Morgan, Ismail Sirageldin, and Nancy Baerwaldt, Productive Americans, (Ann Arbor: Survey Research Center, Monograph No. 43, 1966), p. 79.

2.4.3   Capital income

About 20 percent of the labor force owns a business or farm
and their reported hourly earnings include some return on capital as
well as labor. It is the return on labor which is relevant for our
purpose of imputing the value of unpaid work. Since the allocation of
labor input among the various productive activities depends on its
marginal value product in these various activities, capital income
ought to be subtracted before calculating hourly earnings. Our problem
is how to estimate capital income. Capital income is usually estimated
as some return (5 or 6%) on the total value of investment in the business
or farm: land, building, machines, or livestock. It has been
estimated that the average spending unit received $435 as an imputed
return on investment in an owner-operated farm, or business in 1959.[24]

The value of the business or farm was not available in the 1964
data. Further analysis of the 1959 data, however, indicate that the mean
imputed return on investment in farm or business varied between 47 and 100
percent of the total reported mixed-labor-capital income depending on the
age of the head (Table 2-8). These ratios were used to estimate the
component of total income which was return on the investment. The remaining income realized by the enterprise is considered wages and is added to
the rest of wage income to calculate hourly earnings and estimate the
value of unpaid productive work.[25]

---

[24] Morgan, et. al., Income and Welfare in the United States,
pp. 86-96, 494.

[25] One obvious deficiency in our analysis is that to the extent
that the average capital-labor mix and/or the quality of capital and labor
have changed since 1959; such change will affect the relative return of
labor. Several rough computations show that such changes do not have an
appreciable effect on our estimates of the value or the distribution of
total income.

TABLE 2-8

MEAN MIXED LABOR CAPITAL INCOME AND THE PROPORTION OF IMPUTED INCOME
(RETURN ON REAL INVESTMENT) WITHIN AGE OF HEADS
(for spending units - 1959)

	Mixed Labor - Capital Income		Capital Income as Percent of Mixed Labor-Capital Income
	Mean	(St. Error)	
Age of Head	$	$	%
Under 25	37	16	64
25 - 34	435	121	47
35 - 44	806	120	60
45 - 54	887	124	74
55 - 64	655	130	95
65+	193	100	100
All	536	485	80

2.5   Problems Not Dealt With in the Analysis

The following is essentially a list of problems which are assumed away from our analysis:

1. No account is made for market imperfection on the demand side for labor. To the extent that there are divergences between the value of the marginal product of labor and its market price, reported wages will not reflect real satisfaction or wants. This is partly remedied, however, through our adjustments of the dis-equilibrium situation.

2. No account is taken for the hypothesis that increasing family size is associated with purchase of commodities at quantity rates,[26] which implies that the purchasing power of the same dollar is higher for larger families.

3. We assume that reported average hourly earnings are equal to the marginal wages. This assumes away both monopsony and monopoly power in the labor market. However, hourly earnings are adjusted for marginal Federal tax rates.

2.6   The Procedure Used in the Analysis: a summary

The following is essentially a brief survey of the various manipulation employed to the original data:

a. Market prices: For the Lth unpaid activity in the Kth state calculate:

(1) $\underline{W}_{1k}$ = average market price of labor

b. Opportunity cost:

Given the result of a multivariate analysis on reported hourly earnings or working heads and wives using age, education, sex, and race: Assign hourly earnings for those who did not work. Thus, for the ith individual in the jth family where $i = 1,\ldots, m$ ($m =$ the size of the jth family) and

$j=1, \ldots, n$ ($n =$ the size of the sample = 2214 families), calculate:

---

[26]Martin H. David, Family Composition and Consumption, (Amsterdam: North Holland Publishing Co., 1962) p. 14.

(2) $\underline{W}_{ij}$ = average hourly earnings (reported or assigned);

(3) $\underline{W}^{\circ}_{ij}$ = average adjusted hourly earnings; adjusted for the following:

   (i)   net of capital income

   (ii)   including the time spent on the journey to work (i.e.,

$$W = \frac{\text{Wage Income}}{(\text{Hours of work}) + (\text{Hours of journey to work})}$$

   (iii) net of <u>M</u>arginal <u>T</u>ax <u>R</u>ates (i.e., WX (1-MTR))

   (iv)   adjusted for sickness, unemployment and desired more or less hours of work.

Using these two sets of activity prices, we calculate the value of hours spent on regular housework, home production, volunteer work, education, and the journey to work. Different adjustments for hourly earnings are assumed when we estimate the value of desired more or less hours of work in Chapter 4.

Table 2-9 gives an overall view of the various family income adjustments and imputations made in this study.

TABLE 2-9

INCOME ADJUSTMENTS

Type of Activity or Item		Valuation or Imputation Procedure	Chapter
1. Unpaid Productive Housework	a.	Real costs (Table 2-1)	2,4
Regular housework	b.	Opportunity costs: Using adjusted hourly earnings	
Home production:			
Painting and repairs			
Sewing and mending			
Growing own food			
Canning and freezing			
Other productive activities			
2. Volunteer Work		Opportunity costs: Adjusted hourly earnings	2,4
3. Adult Education		"	4
4. Help Received		Real costs of regular housework (Table 2-1)	2,4
5. Imputed Rent for Home Owners		Net equity X rate of interest	4
6. Imputed Car Services		Net equity X rate of interest	4
7. Potential Income			4
Sickness or unemployment		Unadjusted hourly earnings	
Desired more or less work		Adjusted hourly earnings	

CHAPTER 3

EMPIRICAL CONSIDERATIONS UNDERLYING THE ANALYSIS

3.0   Introduction

It is difficult to discuss validity analysis or more generally
problems of sampling variability in survey data without assuming some
particular focus or purpose. In this study we are mainly concerned
with estimating the distribution and the aggregate value of families'
unpaid work and its impact on the distribution of families' total welfare.
Thus, our concern in this chapter is to assess the validity of the
estimated distributions of families' paid and unpaid hours of work, their
money income, and their demographic and social characteristics which
are essential for any study of economic welfare and its distribution.

3.1   The Sample Used

Data obtained by the Survey Research Center through personal
interview with 2214 adults (representing 2214 families), during January
and February, 1965 are the basis for the analysis in this study. The
data are obtained from a national multi-stage stratified sample of the
contiguous United States. The over-all response rate was about 84
percent and no adjustment was made for non-response. The interviews
were clustered in each of the 74 primary sampling units.[1] Indeed,

---

[1] For detailed discussion of the definitions and methodology used
in the Survey Research Center's samples, see: Leslie Kish and Irene Hess,
The Survey Research Center's National Sample of Dwellings, (Ann Arbor:
Institute for Social Research, The University of Michigan, 1965). See also,
James Morgan et. al., Productive Americans (Ann Arbor: Institute for
Social Research, The University of Michigan, 1966), pp. 360-78.

the effect of clustering is to underestimate the variance in the data
if methods which assume simple random sampling are used.[2]

3.2   Sampling Variability[3]

Sample statistics calculated from Survey data are subject to
errors arising from several sources. This is the case since social
surveys involve many operations and every one of them is subject to
error. A convenient classification, however, of survey errors could
be presented as follows:

$$(1) \qquad y_i = Y_i + \left[\sum_r B_r^* + \sum_k B_k \right] + \left[\sum_s V_{is}^* + \sum_e V_{ie} \right]$$

$$(2) \qquad y_i - Y_i = \left[\sum_r B_r^* + \sum_k B_k \right] + \left[\sum_s V_{is}^* + \sum_e V_{ie} \right]$$

$$(3) \qquad E\left((\bar{y}) - \bar{Y} \right) = \left[\sum_r B_r^* + \sum_k B_k \right] + \left[0 + E(\bar{V}_{ie}) \right]$$

where:

y_i = the ith individual's observed or measured value

Y_i = the true value

---

[2] In this 1965 Survey, clustering of neighboring dwellings was
reduced from approximately four per cluster to two or three on the average.
The expected result is some moderate reduction in sampling variability,
ibid, 360.

[3] The discussion in this section is very brief. For a detailed
analysis of sampling variability see Chapter 13 of Leslie Kish, Survey
Sampling (New York: John Wiley & Sons, Inc., 1965). See also, Hansen,
Hurwitz and Madow (1953, II, ch. 12) or Kendall and Stuart (1966, III,
ch. 39).

B_r^* = sampling bias: a sampling error due to the rth source but constant for all elements such as:

    a. Frame biases in the selection procedures

    b. Constant statistical bias which could be reduced through the use of proper statistical estimation procedures (e.g., using the median as an estimate of the mean of a skewed distribution).

B_k = Non sampling bias: sampling errors constant for all elements such as:

    a. Non coverage

                   } Non observation

    b. Non response

    c. Field data collection

                 } Observation

    d. Office processing

V_{is}^* = Sampling variable errors that depend on the survey design. For example, the variance of a mean based on a design involving three stages of random selection with replacement from equal clusters =

$$V\ (\bar{y})\ =\ \frac{S_a^2}{a}\ +\ \frac{S_b^2}{ab}\ +\ \frac{S_c^2}{abc}$$

where a = primary sampling units;

        ab = second stage units, and

        n = abc = elements selected in the final stage.

    (Kish, 1965, ch. 13)

V_{ie} = Nonsampling variable errors

In the 1965 survey, processing errors are thought to be negligible because of careful checks built into the analysis. In general, response and reporting errors are reasonably small and will be discussed in the next section. Sampling variability errors on the other hand are affected by the survey design. Taking account of the design effect, standard errors for some important sample statistics for major groups of the sample were computed and reported elsewhere (Morgan, 1966). Variances estimated by assuming simple random sampling design could be adjusted by a factor (K_i) to account for the design effect. In that study, K_i was found to be a simple linear function of the number of sample cases (n_i) in the base of the sample statistic.

$$(4) \qquad K_i = 1.4 + .0007 \ n_i$$

In this study the same adjustment factor is used whenever standard errors are calculated.[4] The following formulas are used (Kish and Hess, 1965, 48-53).

---

[4] The aim of a sample design is to reduce estimation variance as much as possible given some total cost constraints. Clustering tends to reduce cost per element since the number of independent selections is reduced but at the expense of increasing the estimation variance. The estimation variance, however, could be reduced through stratified sampling at increased costs. A typical survey design problem is an economic one: to minimize a cost function through optimal mix of clustering and stratification for a given sample size or total cost and survey objective. The effect of the sample design on the sampling variability for a given statistic for a subgroup of the sample will depend on the actual mix of clustering and stratification, on the type of variable analyzed, and on the size of the base of the statistic. For an estimated statistic for a given variable, the larger the subsample considered the greater the effect of clustering will tend to be. (i.e., K_i will be greater).

(5)   The standard error of a mean (or a ratio)

$$r_i = \sqrt{var\ (r_i)} = \sqrt{K_i\ \frac{(SD)^2}{n_i}}$$

Var (r_i) = variance of r_i for the present sample

(6)   The standard error of the difference of two statistics r_1 and r_2 is <u>approximated</u> by the formula

$$SE\ (\ r_1 - r_2\ ) = \sqrt{Var\ (r_1) + Var\ (r_2)}$$

3.3   Validity of the Data

There are three ways one can assess the accuracy of survey data. First, aggregates, distributions, or overall proportions could be estimated and compared with official government estimates. There are some indications that the survey of the Economic Behavior Program (EBP) upon which this book was based finds fewer low-income single-person units and finds more high-income units than are found in official estimates by the U.S. Bureau of Census (Table 3-1).[5] This might be a result of using somewhat different concepts of family units. Also, the EBP survey might be missing roomers and boarders who usually have low incomes. Furthermore it gets more detailed and probably more complete income information, which accounts for some of the income differences.

---

[5] The Economic Behavior Program (EBP) is part of the Institute for Social Research, the University of Michigan.

The implications for our analysis might not be of first importance since our main interest is in the relative welfare positions of families with sufficient economic independence and since many of the unrelated individuals missed by the EBP are young people (less than 18 years of age) and are not considered adults in the EBP definition.

More important is the fact that there are no official estimates of time allocation to compare with the EBP estimate. This leads us to the second way of assessing the accuracy of survey data namely by checking against another survey done by a different agency or at a different time.

In 1966, the Political Behavior Program of the Survey Research Center of the Institute for Social Research did a national study of time use of the United States' urban population as a part of an international study across eleven widely different countries. It is rather comforting that the estimate of time use in the two studies are rather close in spite of differences in concepts, coverage, and methods of interviewing.[6]

In the 1964 EBP survey, information about productive use of time was obtained by asking several simple questions that do not require hour and minute details by types of activities, e.g., on the average about how much of your time is spent working around the house?), since the main focus was not on detailed time-budget analysis but rather on time allocation among broadly defined activities. And several pretests with

---

[6] See the extensive analysis and evaluation of the two studies by John Robinson, The Workday, (mimeo), Institute for Social Research, The University of Michigan, 1967. See also John P. Robinson and Philip E. Converse, 66 Basic Tables on Time-Budget Data for the United States, Monograph, Institute for Social Research, The University of Michigan, 1966.

TABLE 3-1

DISTRIBUTION OF FAMILY INCOME WITHIN FAMILY SIZE (1964)

(for Survey of Consumer Finances and Current Population Survey)

Number of People in Family

	One		Two		Three		Four	
Family Income	SCF	CPS	SCF	CPS	SCF	CPS	SCF	CPS
Under $1,000	12.0	26.0	3.6	4.6	2.0	3.0	2.3	2.0
$1000-1999	18.9	24.3	9.3	11.2	5.4	4.7	6.7	3.3
$2000-2999	18.6	12.2	10.2	12.9	5.9	7.0	5.0	4.6
$3000-3999	8.6	8.9	10.4	10.9	7.8	7.8	6.3	6.0
$4000-4999	7.1	8.5	7.9	9.4	6.8	9.3	6.0	7.7
$5000-5999	9.1	6.6	8.9	9.3	10.5	10.5	7.8	10.3
$6000-9999	18.8	10.3	27.5	24.9	33.6	34.5	39.6	38.7
$10,000 - 14,999	8.1	1.8	14.3	12.5	20.6	16.9	16.7	19.6
$15,000 and over	5.9	1.3	7.8	4.4	7.4	6.4	9.6	8.0
Total	100.1	99.9	99.9	100.1	100.0	100.1	100.0	100.2
Percent of families	16.7	20.1	28.7	26.2	16.6	16.8	17.3	15.3

(Table 3-1 continued Page 49)

TABLE 3-1 (continued)

DISTRIBUTION OF FAMILY INCOME WITHIN FAMILY SIZE (1964)

(for Survey of Consumer Finances and Current Population Survey)

Number of People in Family

Family Income	Five SCF	Five CPS	Six SCF	Six CPS	Seven or more SCF	Seven or more CPS	All Families SCF	All Families CPS
Under $1,000	1.6	2.1	3.3	2.7	1.7	3.0	4.2	7.8
$1000-1999	6.4	2.8	6.0	3.1	6.1	5.5	9.2	9.9
$2000-2999	4.0	4.8	2.7	5.0	10.1	7.7	7.7	8.9
$3000-3999	5.3	7.0	7.7	5.9	4.5	9.7	8.0	8.5
$4000-4999	9.1	6.9	9.9	8.1	7.8	9.0	7.5	8.6
$5000-5999	10.4	9.8	10.4	10.1	11.2	10.2	9.3	9.2
$6000-9999	32.8	39.6	34.0	37.8	39.1	34.4	30.5	28.5
$10,000 - 14,999	20.0	19.0	14.8	19.5	14.0	14.0	15.3	13.3
$15,000 and over	10.4	8.0	11.0	7.7	5.0	6.4	8.0	5.3
Total	100.0	100.0	99.8	99.9	99.5	100.0	99.7	100.0
Percent of families	10.7	10.4	5.1	5.5	4.9	5.7	100.0	100.0

Source: U.S. Bureau of the Census, Current Population Reports, Series P-60, No. 47. "Income in 1964 of Families and Persons in the United States,", U.S. Government Printing Office, Washington, D.C., 1966.

various degrees of required details suggested that the interviewing time increases and the quality and quantity of total information required (i.e., time use, financial, attitudinal, and demographic data) decline as more details on time use were asked.

The Time use survey conducted by the Political Behavior Program (PBP) used an elaborate diary procedure. Interviewers were required to (a) take a short (20-25 minute) preliminary interview with the respondent, (b) explain the diary to the respondent and leave the diary with him (her), (c) return at least one day later to complete or correct portions of the diary with the respondent and complete the remaining portions of the questionnaire. Table 3-2 compares weekly time spent on housework for various subgroups of the population as estimated from the two studies. With the exception of married men, our time estimates were higher in all cases. One reason is the sample coverage. The Political Behavior Program study did not include the rural population, who tend to spend more time around the house. Also, the age distribution differed between the two studies with relatively more young heads of families (less than 35 years) in the PBP sample. Other reasons are clearly related to different methods of interviewing or to differences in the definition of housework. The important point, however, is that in spite of all those possible reasons for expected difference, none of the results of the two studies differed by more than 10 to 20 percent for any of the important subgroups of the sample. The overall average differed by less than 5 percent. Furthermore, for the purpose of isolating difference in individual welfare it seems that our data are more adequate in terms of coverage and general validity on other income and demographic variables.

The third way of assessing the accuracy of survey data is to rely upon the care and precision with which the survey was conducted. It's widely acknowledged that surveys conducted by the Survey Research Center of the University of Michigan are carefully designed and conducted.

TABLE 3-2

WEEKLY HOURS SPENT ON REGULAR HOUSEWORK

	PBP	EBP
Single Men	7.3	7.8
Married Men	9.1	3.7
Single Women (no children)	16.7	20.3
Single Women (with children)	29.8	34.3
Married Women (no children)	27.2	31.9
Married Women (children 4 or more)	35.5	39.7
Married Women (one pre-school child)	38.8	43.0
Married Women (more than one pre-school child)	46.9	54.6
Total	22.0	22.8

Source: John Robinson, The Workday, (mimeo), Institute for Social Research, The University of Michigan, 1967.

3.4   A Note on the Tables

The various estimates of family income components imputed in this study are classified by different demographic characteristics. Means and medians are given for each classification and for aggregates. An attempt has been made to evaluate the explanatory power of each classification (i.e., each table), the significance of such classification, and the stability of the estimated means. The intra-class correlation coefficient, F-ratios, and standard errors adjusted for the sample design are computed for most of the tables in Chapter 4.[7]

---

[7] The intra-class correlation coefficient is defined as the ratio of the estimate of the components of variance explained by the classification and the total variance. See George W. Snedecor, Statistical Methods Applied to Experiments in Agriculture and Biology (5th ed.; Ames, The Collegiate Press, 1956), pp. 257-285.

CHAPTER 4

FAMILIES' FULL AND POTENTIAL INCOME: 1964

In a subject where there is no agreed procedure for
knocking out errors, doctrines have a long life[1]

4.0   Introduction

In 1964, the average value of unpaid output for the American

family is estimated at $3,929 or about 50 percent of its disposable

income. This is indeed a substantial sum. Its exclusion from the

---

[1]   Joan Robinson, Economic Philosophy, (Chicago: Aldine
Publishing Co., 1963), p. 75. It seems like unbroken tradition
among economists even of present times to follow Adam Smith's notion
of classing domestic help and servants as unproductive: "... thus the
labour of a manufacturer adds, generally, to the value of the materials
which he works upon, that of his own maintenance, and of his master's
profit. The labour of a menial servant, on the contrary, adds to the
value of nothing", The Wealth of Nations (New York: The Modern Library,
1937), p. 314.
        Alfred Marshall, however, strongly criticized Adam's distinction
between productive and unproductive labor: "...there is no distinction
in character between the work of the baker who provides bread for a
family and that of the cook who boils potatoes". Marshall also defined
labour as "...any exertion of mind or body undergone partly or wholly
with a view to some good other than the pleasure derived directly from
the work", and stressed the ambiguous meaning of productive since
"...consumption is the end of production", Alfred Marshall, Principles
of Economics (8th ed., London: Macmillan & Co. LTD.,1920), pp. 55-57.
        This old rooted distinction is partly responsible for the futile
controversies that have arisen with the initiation of the statistics of
national income on the question whether or not government output should
be considered a part of national product. For a critical review of the
controversy, see Joseph A. Schumpeter, History of Economic Analysis,
(New York: Oxford University Press, 1954), pp. 628-631.
        Presently,the value of government output is included in the
official national accounts but not the value of housework or home production. And typical current text books discussion usually dismiss the
issue either by a joke or by recognizing the problem but indicating the
serious difficulties associated with its measurement. See for example,
Gardner Ackley, Macroeconomic Theory (New York: The Macmillan & Co.LTD.,
1961), p. 55-57.

national accounts might cause serious biases when comparisons of
levels or rates of growth are made among countries or over time.

About 90 percent of the estimated unpaid production is in the
form of housework and other types of home production. The rest consists
of volunteer work (5 percent), time spent on education by heads of
families (3 percent), and service income received from the family's
car(s). Also a family received an average of $18 worth of free help
from friends and relatives.[2] (See Table 4-1).

In this chapter we first examine the distribution of full income,
defined as the sum of disposable income and total unpaid output, by
various demographic characteristics. Second, a brief discussion of the
various components of full income is given, and finally we introduce
the concept of "potential income". Potential income adds to full income
an estimate of the value of output lost because of sickness or unemployment and adjusts for the desire of working family heads for more or
fewer hours of work (i.e., what is the level and distribution of total
family income if everyone is healthy, employed and satisfied with the
allocation of his time between work and leisure?).

The analysis in this chapter which focuses on alternative
measures of income thus sets the stage for the discussion of income
inequality and the distribution of welfare in Chapter 5.

---

[2] All estimated values of unpaid productive activities discussed
in this and the following chapters are based on the opportunity cost
approach unless otherwise indicated. Real cost estimates are discussed
and compared with opportunity cost estimates in section 4.2 below. For
a theoretical discussion of the real and opportunity cost approaches,
see section 2.2 above.

TABLE 4-1

MEANS AND MEDIANS OF FULL AND POTENTIAL FAMILY INCOME

Concept of Family Income	Median	Mean*	Percent With Such Income
	(dollars)		
1. DI: Family Disposable Income including imputed rent for home owners	6400	8115 (1300)	100%
+ [Housework + Home Production]	3050	3523 (182)	91
2. [DI + HW]		11638 (1396)	100
+ Volunteer work	140	204 (82)	56
+ Education of heads of families		141 (40)	5
+ Value of the family's car(s) services		44 (12)	84
+ Free help received by the family		18	5
3. FI: Family Full Income	10250	12045 (1306)	100
+ Value of time lost because of sickness or unemployment		500 (92)	26
+ Value of desired more or fewer hours of work by heads of families		92 (24)	36
4. PI: Potential Income	9200	12638 (1310)	100

* Standard errors are given in parenthesis beside the means.

4.1   Full Family Income

Full family income is defined as the sum of families' disposable
income, the value of unpaid productive activities done or received by
family members, and the value of families' car(s) services. Alternatively
it could be defined as total market and non-market economic resources
at the disposal of the income-consumer-welfare units (i.e., family units).

Total family money income data were obtained in 1965, through
the standard Survey of Consumer Finances procedure, on the basis of a
series of questionnaire items which included separate questions about
income received by the head of the family and also by other family members.
Data on wages, business income, salaries, income from farming, professional
practice, rent, interest, dividends, social security, pensions, and
from other forms of transfer payments were obtained for the head and his
wife separately. Further questions elicited information about the
incomes of other family members.[3]

Federal income taxes were estimated for each family unit and subtracted to obtain disposable income. Estimated disposable income is the

[3] Information about family income in 1964 are presented in,
George Katona, C.A. Lininger, and E. Mueller, 1964 Survey of Consumer
Finances, (Ann Arbor: Survey Research Center, The University of Michigan,
1965), pp. 3-24; 227-230. For a detailed discussion and a critical
evaluation of income data obtained by the Survey Research Center, see
T. Paul Schultz, The Distribution of Personal Income, Joint Economic
Committee, Congress of the United States, 88th. Congress, 2nd sess.
(December, 1964), pp. 73-77. See also Sirken and Others, "The Survey
of Consumer Finances and the Census Quality Check," in An Appraisal
of the 1950 Census Income Data, Studies in Income and Wealth, vol. 23,
National Bureau of Economic Research, Princeton University Press, 1958,
pp. 165-167.

basic income data used in this study.[4]

In the following analysis, net rent from owner-occupied dwellings were estimated as 6 percent of the present net equity of the house and included as part of families' disposable income.[5]

---

[4] As mentioned before in Chapter 3, the sample of the Survey Research Center may exclude a disproportionate number of the two extremes of the income distribution (i.e., the lower as well as the higher income groups) which are important in an analysis of the distribution of disposable income. Whenever possible, medians as well as means will be presented as a measure of the central value of the size distribution since medians are less sensitive than means to sampling variability in the estimation of the extremes of the distribution.

[5] The Survey data used in this study did not have information about imputed net rent for home owners. However, for purposes of comparing welfare, the exclusion of imputed net rent for home owners will under estimate the real welfare of home owners especially for the aged where homes constitute most of their net worth, and have the greatest equity since they are all paid for. (The fact that most older people have more housing than they need is discussed in Chapter 5). In order to impute net rent we need information about the net equity of the home (market value minus mortgage value). However, we only had information about market house values but not about home mortgages.

Fortunately, a parallel national sample by the Survey of Consumer Finances did include information about home mortgages. The following steps have been done to estimate rent for home owners:

    a. A multivariate analysis was done using the value of home mortgage as a dependent variable and house value, age of head, and the number of years lived in the house as predictors. The results (see Table 4-2) were used to estimate mortgage values for home owners.

    b. The estimated mortgage values from step (1) were then multiplied by the probability of home owners to have a mortgage. The latter varied between 10 and 93 percent depending on the family's stage in the life cycle (Table 4-3).

Footnote continued next page

Footnote 5 continued

TABLE 4-2

MULTIVARIATE ANALYSIS OF HOME MORTGAGES
(Means of Total Mortgage by House Value, Age of Head, and
Number of Years in the House)

Present Value of the House	Age of Head 45 or More				Age of Head Less than 45 Years			
	Lived in the House for 10 Years or More		Lived in the House for Less than 10 Years		Lived 5 Years or More in the House		Lived Less than 5 Years in the House	
	Mtg.	St.Err.*	Mtg.	St.Err.	Mtg.	St.Err.	Mtg.	St.Err.
Under $2500	000	---	136	156	988	1078	988	1078
2500-4999	196	392	669	370	1211	475	1211	475
5000-7499	196	392	1607	644	2195	577	2195	577
7500-9999	554	199	1892	689	4473	613	4473	613
10,000-12,499	684	284	4084	890	6317	743	6317	743
12,500-14,499	1816	460	4072	1028	7658	918	7658	918
14,500-19,999	1816	460	5823	1362	7871	818	12,784	683
20,000-24,999	2351	784	5823	1362	8903	1397	17,011	942
25,000 or more	3085	794	10,773	2449	10,450	1796	17,770	1936

* See Chapter 3 for a discussion of estimating standard errors.
$(R^2 = .48)$

TABLE 4-3

WHETHER HAVE A MORTGAGE BY LIFE CYCLE IN 1964

Stage in the Life Cycle	Percent Having a Mortgage
Under 45, single, no children	50%*
Under 45, married, no children	50*
Under 45, married child under 6	93
Under 45, married, child 6 or older	88
45 or older, married, children	65
45 or older, married, no children, in labor force	48
45 or older, married, no children retired	22
45 or older, single, in labor force	37
45 or older, single, retired	10
45 or older, single, children	10*

* Fewer than 50 cases.

Source: Survey Research Center, "Housing", Statistical Report Number III, 1965 Survey of Consumer Finances, Economic Behavior Program.

Footnote continued next page

4.1.1 The determinants of full income

In our previous discussions[6], we assumed that the family,
given its preference function and its basic constraints (i.e., supply
conditions) and given the market and institutional constraints (i.e.,
demand conditions), makes a set of interrelated decisions that could be
interpreted as a set of sequential decisions. First, a decision is
made about the type and amount of market activities done by the various
members of the family that determines its total money income. Second,
a decision is made about the type and amount of nonmarket activities that

---

Footnote 5 continued

    c. Estimated mortgages from step 2 were subtracted from the
reported market house values and the resultant net equities
were multiplied by 6 percent to estimate imputes net rents.
Farmers reported, a combined estimate of the values of their
farms and homes. There was no way to estimate separately
the value of their homes. In such cases, house values were
taken at 30 percent of their reported value and imputed
rents were calculated as usual.

There is no way to assess the reliability of our procedure as
compared with that of the U.S. Department of Commerce. Since the latter
reports that:

"the rent estimate continues to be among the least
satisfactory component of the national income statistics.
This condition is largely a reflection of the heter-
ogeneity, poor statistical quality, and serious gaps which
characterize the basic data at many points".

U.S. Department of Commerce, Office of Business Economics, U.S. Income
and Output: A Supplement to the Survey of Current Business, U.S.
Government Office, Washington, D.C., 1958, p. 93.

[6] See section 2.2 above.

determines its full income as well as the type and amount of its consumptive and leisure activities.[7] Consumptive and leisure activities require both time and goods and services whether produced at home or purchased in the market.

Families with low money incomes tend to produce more at home either to achieve or to improve a given level or quality of consumption. But low money income could be a result of low hourly earnings or a result of constraints on possible hours of work. On the other hand, the desire to increase non-market production is related to the family's present and expected needs relative to its present and expected money income as well as to the dynamics of its level of aspirations. The latter is related to past experiences and to various background factors.[8]

The forgoing argument suggest three rather general hypotheses:

Hypothesis 1: Families' "full income" will be more equally distributed than families' "disposable income". Since families with lower money income tend to produce relatively more non-market output.

Hypothesis 2: Increasing family size is associated with more non-market production since family consumption increases faster than family income as family size increases.[9]

Hypothesis 3: Age, education, family structure, and race are important determinants of families' "full income". But there are significant interactions between them since past experiences and expected behavior will differ depending on the various combinations of those demographic variables.

---

[7] For example, people with low money incomes will tend to choose consumptive or leisure activities that are either labor intensive (e.g., walking, sight seeing, watching television) or those which require more non-market goods and services (e.g., build own boat).

[8] James N. Morgan, I. Sirageldin, N. Baerwaldt, Productive Americans, p. 458-460.

[9] Martin H. David, Family Composition and Consumption, (Amsterdam: North Holland Publishing Co., 1962), p. 14.

4.1.2   The distribution of full income

The addition of non-market income to disposable income reduces the degree of income inequality. Table 4-4 shows the distributions of disposable income (including net imputed rent), disposable income plus housework, and full income.

A simple measure of a distribution's skewness is the ratio of the mean to the median. If the mean-median ratio was 1, the distribution would be symmetrical about the mode. Ratios in excess of 1 indicate increasing skewness of the distribution, and are associated with increasing relative inequality and dispersion.[10] The mean-median ratio were 1.27 for disposable income and 1.17 for full income : a reduction of 8 percent.

The Lorenz curve provides another convenient tool for presenting the size distribution of income (see Figure 4-1). Income recipients are placed in ascending order on the horizontal axis, while income is cumulated on the vertical axis. The diagonal line signifies "perfect equality". The area between the curve and the line, if expressed as a proportion of the lower triangle, results in a useful statistic, R, the concentration ratio. Zero represents complete equality; 1.0 represents the concentration of all income in the hand of one unit.[11] The concentration ratio R is .40 and .37 for disposable incomes (including imputed rent) and full family income respectively.

---

[10] See J. Aitchison and J.A.C. Brown, The Lognormal Distribution, (Cambridge: Cambridge University Press, 1963), pp. 8-13 and pp. 154-155.

[11] "For a discussion of various measures of inequality see, Hayward R. Alker, Jr. and Bruce M. Russel, "On Measuring Inequality", Behavioral Science, 9 (July, 1964) pp. 207-218.

FIGURE 4-1

LORENZ CURVE

FULL FAMILY INCOME AND DISPOSABLE INCOME, 1964

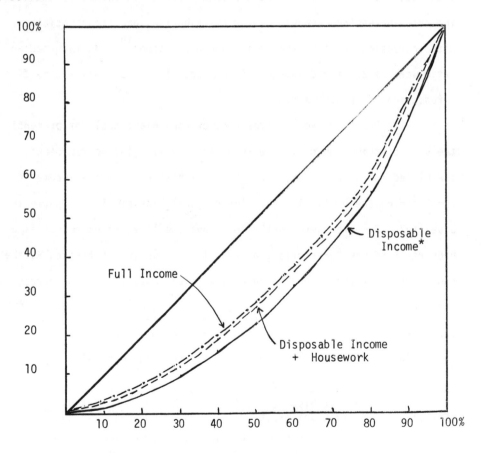

Cumulative Percentage
of Dollars

Cumulative Percentage of Families

_____

* Includes imputed rent

TABLE 4-4

DISTRIBUTIONS, MEANS, AND MEDIANS OF FULL
AND DISPOSABLE FAMILY INCOME, 1964
(for all 2214 families)

Income Brackets	Disposable Income		Disposable Income and Housework		Full Income	
	Percent of Cases	Mean*	Percent of Cases	Mean*	Percent of Cases	Mean*
Less than $2,000	12%	$ 1,298 (43)	2%	$ 1,388 (105)	2%	$ 1.378 (111)
$2,000 - 3,499	12	2,754 (40)	6	2,790 (60)	5	2,815 (61)
$3,500 - 4,999	12	4,248 (41)	7	4,250 (57)	7	4,242 (48)
$5,000 - 6,499	14	5,740 (37)	10	5,723 (45)	8	5,746 (47)
$6,500 - 7,999	15	7,240 (35)	11	7,264 (47)	11	7,253 (49)
$8,000 - 9,499	11	8,704 (43)	12	8,760 (42)	12	8,771 (43)
$9,500 - 10,999	7	10,254 (45)	12	10,245 (42)	11	10,232 (44)
$11,000-12,999	7	11,861 (71)	12	11,919 (55)	13	11,917 (53)
$13,000-14,999	3	14,049 (109)	10	13,919 (75)	9	13,917 (60)
$15,000 or more	7	35,137 (3,888)	18	24,971 (4,293)	22	24,271 (5,192)
Total Mean	100	8,115 (650)	100	11,638 (648)	100	12,045 (653)
Median		6,400		9,410		10,250
Ratio of Mean to Median		1.27		1.21		1.17

* Standard errors are given in parenthesis under the means.

Table 4-5 shows the relation of full income and its components to total family money income. The absolute value of families non-market income does not vary much between money income brackets so its <u>relative</u> importance varies inversely with money income. Families with less than $1,000 money incomes more than tripled that income through housework and home production. The effect of that behavior on the distribution of income becomes more apparent when the ratio of the mean value of home production to disposable income is plotted against the log of total family money income, (Figure 4-2). This apparent significant correlation suggests that people faced with constraints in their market activities strive to improve their standards of living (or to maintain a decent life) by increasing their non-market productive activities. Also the fact that high income families tend to do relatively less of such activities means that if one included the value of leisure, the distribution of welfare would be altered in the other direction (toward more inequality), since the higher the income, the more free time (except at the very top among the professionals and executives).

4.1.3   Full income among population groups

About 10 percent of heads of American families were either retired or housewives over fifty-five years of age (more than half of them were single people). In the following analysis, they will be treated as a separate group and our attention will be given to examine the effect

TABLE 4-5

FULL INCOME, DISPOSABLE INCOME AND HOUSEWORK,
AND DISPOSABLE INCOME BY TOTAL MONEY INCOME, 1964

Total Money Income Brackets*	Disposable Income	Disposable Income and Housework	Full Income	Ratio of Non-market Income to Money Income	Number of Cases
Less than $1,000	867	$2,890	$3,325	284 %	100
$1,000-1,999	2,686	5,506	6,095	127	204
$2,000-2,999	2,674	5,812	6,455	141	163
$3,000-3,999	3,666	6,875	7,334	100	175
$4,000-4,999	4,535	7,588	8,169	80	156
$5,000-5,999	5,436	9,061	9,581	76	194
$6,000-7,499	6,575	9,939	10,585	61	304
$7,500-9,999	8,216	11,835	12,517	52	395
$10,000-14,999	11,147	14,780	15,531	39	341
$15,000 or more	29,817	32,958	33,727	13	181
All Families	8,115	11,638	12,045	48 %	2,214
Fc (Calculated F. ratio)	21.00	22.00	22.00		
F.01	2.52	2.52	2.52		
R^2	.28	.29	.29		

*Before taxes and excluding imputed net rents.

FIGURE 4-2

THE RATIO OF NON-MARKET INCOME TO DISPOSABLE
INCOME BY TOTAL FAMILY MONEY INCOME
(For all 2214 families)

Value of Unpaid Work
as Percent of Disposable Income

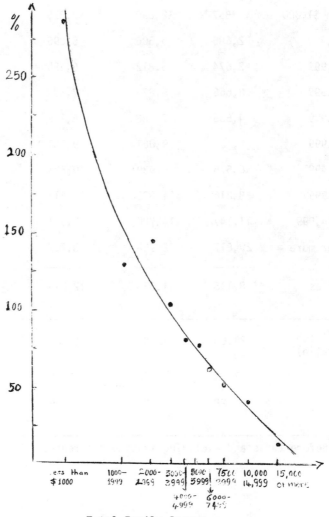

Total Family Income
(Log Scale)

of various factors on the distribution of full income for the rest of
the population, namely, the effect of family size, race, age and education.[12]

(a)   Family size

Larger families tend to have high non-market income relative
to disposable income (Figure 4-3). The notion that money income does
not increase as fast as family size is illustrated in Table 4-6. The
case of one-person families illustrates clearly the hypothesis that it
is the combined effect of the family's needs and its means that determine
its full income. One would expect, that on the basis of family size
alone, one-person families would have lower non-market income (e.g.,
they have smaller homes with no children to care for). On the other hand,
given that their disposable income is the lowest of the family size
groups (mostly students or working females), one would expect relatively
higher non-market income. In fact evidence in Figure 4-3 and Table 4-6
suggests that these two forces (family size and money income) have operated
to yield an intermediate outcome: non-market income is higher than one
would expect solely on the basis of family size and lower than one would
expect solely on the basis of money income.

---

[12] The study of the factors that determine the income distribution
of the retired is essential for any serious study of national welfare.
However, the size of the present sample and the scope of this study do not
permit such analysis. For a recent contribution that examines critically
the economic position of the retired, see George Katona and James Morgan,
"Retired in Prospect and Retrospect", (Mimeo), Survey Research Center, The
Unviersity of Michigan, 1967.

FIGURE 4-3

THE RATIO OF NON-MARKET INCOME TO DISPOSABLE
INCOME BY FAMILY SIZE, 1964
(For 1803 families: not retired heads of families or
not housewives 55 or older)

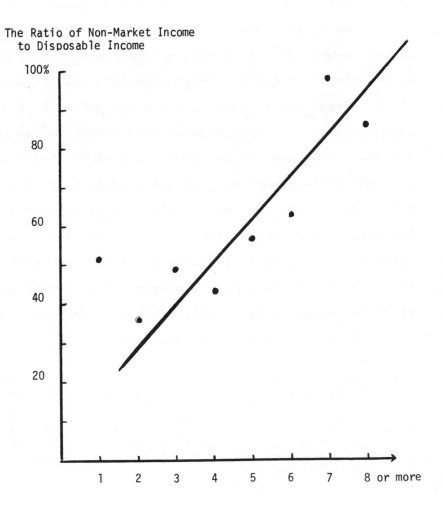

Number of People in the Family

TABLE 4-6

FULL AND DISPOSABLE INCOME BY FAMILY SIZE

(For 1803 families whose heads were not
retired or were not housewives 55 or older)

Number of People in the Family	Means of Income		Number of Cases
	Disposable Income	Full Income	
One person	$ 4,524	$ 6,828	206
Two	10,133	13,818	445
Three	8,036	11,995	343
Four	9,490	13,724	377
Five	9,065	14,251	217
Six	8,210	13,302	105
Seven	6,603	13,219	50
Eight or more	7,537	14,057	59
All	8,534	12,666	1803

(b)   Race

Racial discrimination has been of academic and public interest for several years. Whether the social and economic position of the American Negroes has been improving is a matter of academic debate.[13] In 1964, the average disposable income of a Negro family was about 52 percent of that of a white family. However, the Negro family increased its income by 82 percent through non-market production as compared to 43 percent for the white family. Thus, the income differential is reduced by 12 percent. Furthermore, when we estimate "potential income" which accounts for income lost because of unemployment or sickness as well as for the desires for more or fewer hours of work, the result is a further reduction in the income differential (Figure 4-4).[14] The remaining income differential reflects the present distribution of education and skills between the two races that could be related to past discrimination.

(c)   Age and education

Current income is partly a result of past decisions, partly a result of luck and current circumstances, and partly a result of native ability and other factors uncontrolled by the individual. Within the same educational groups, there exist some lifetime differences in earnings as a result of differences in age. Also people in the same age groups experience various degrees of fluctuations in their incomes as a result

---

[13] See for example, Alan B. Batchelder, "Decline in the Relative Income of Negro Men", The Quarterly Journal of Economics, LXXVIII (November 1966). Also, G.S. Becker, The Economics of Discrimination (Chicago: University of Chicago Press, 1957), and Elton Rayack, "Discrimination and the Occupational Progress of Negroes", Review of Economics and Statistics, XLIII (May 1961), pp. 209-14.

[14] Potential income is discussed in 4.3 below.

FIGURE 4-4

MEAN FULL AND POTENTIAL INCOME BY RACE

(For 1762 families who are either white or Negro,
non-retired, and not housewives 55 or older)

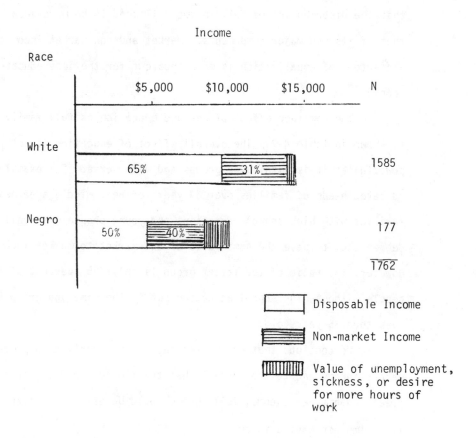

of illness, unemployment, or other temporary events that are related to
their levels of education.

The hypothesis that people supplement their money income through
variations in their non-market production implies that there exist a
non-zero covariance between market and non-market incomes. But since
the incidence of short run fluctuations is probably highly uneven among
the low educated especially the young[15], one would expect in general,
that the distribution of full income will tend to be more equal than
that of its two major components: market and non-market incomes, but
the extent of equalization is more apparent for the less educated young
people.[16]

The combined effect of age and education on full family income
is shown in Table 4-7. The overall effect of education is not as
powerful as it is within age groups and vice versa. For example, low
educated heads of families over 64 years of age, middle aged heads of
families with high school education, and young people with college
degree seem to have the same ratio of non-market to market income.
However, the ratio of the latter group is only 55 percent of that of
people without high school education but in the same age group (i.e.,
less than 35 years old).

We conclude that non-market income is clearly a supplement to
earned income and to the extent that the family could adjust it more
freely than money income, full income could be used as a proxy for
life time per capita income.

---

[15] During periods of depressions, "the least productive or socially
desirable workers are the first made jobless in the cyclical downturn",
T.Paul Shultz, The Distribution of Personal Income, Joint Committee Print
of the U.S. Joint Economic Committee, 88th Cong., 2nd. Sess. (Dec. 1964),
p. 28. See also Morgan, and Others, Income and Welfare in the United States,

[16] See, however, the discussion of full income in Chapter 5 below.

TABLE 4-7

FULL INCOME AND ITS COMPONENT WITHIN AGE
AND EDUCATIONAL GROUPS, 1964

(for 1803 families whose heads were non-retired
or housewives 55 or older)

| Education | Age | | | |
	Less than 35	35 - 64	65 or Older	All Ages
Less than 12 grades				
$ Mean Disposable Income (DI)	$ 4,780	7,023	6,511	6,614
$ Mean Full Income (FI)	8,806	10,849	9,705	10,433
Ratio of market to non-market Income	86%	54%	49%	56%
Percent of cases	7%	33%	3%	43%
12 Grades, No college degree				
$ Mean Disposable Income (DI)	$ 6,136	9,294	7,614	8,156
$ Mean Full Income (FI)	10,556	13,845	10,113	12,608
Ratio of market to non-market income	72%	49%	33%	54%
Percent of cases	15%	27%	*	44%
College Degree				
$ Mean Disposable Income (DI)	$ 8,414	20,407	18,735	15,948
$ Mean Full Income (FI)	12,340	24,664	22,102	20,057
Ratio of market Income	47%	21%	18%	26%
Percent of cases	5%	8%	*	13%
All Educational Groups Ratio of market to non-market income	68%	44%	38%	48%

---

*Fewer than 50 cases.

4.2   The Components of Non-Market Income: the effect of different methods of valuation

4.2.1   The value of housework and home production: opportunity costs versus real costs

Until now, we reported those estimates of non-market income that were based on the opportunity cost approach. Real costs or market prices have been also used to estimate the value of housework and home production that comprise 90 percent of all non-market income. Those estimated values (based on market prices) were $459 lower (i.e., 12 percent lower) than those based on the opportunity cost approach. Market price estimates, however, were higher than the opportunity cost estimates for low income people and much lower for high income people (Figure 4-5). This apparent difference is mainly a result of differences in hourly earnings. Table 4-8 shows the difference between the two sets of estimates within age and educational groups: the mean difference increases with higher levels of education. Accordingly, the use of the market price estimates will probably cause a further reduction in the inequality of full income.

More important, however, is the question of which of the two estimates better reflects the true value of non-market production. We argue that for purposes of comparing welfare, the opportunity costs are more adequate measures of the true value of such activities to the individuals. But from the national point of view, the difference between both estimates is an important number. To the extent that market values are adequate estimates of non-market output, then the difference between estimates based on opportunity costs and market prices reflects existing misallocation of resources since total output could be increased with more specialization. This argument suggests that if people are not faced

FIGURE 4-5

MEAN DIFFERENCE BETWEEN OPPORTUNITY COST AND
MARKET PRICE ESTIMATES OF THE VALUE OF HOUSEWORK
AND HOME PRODUCTION BY FULL FAMILY INCOME, 1964

(For 1803 families whose heads were not retired
  or not housewives 55 or older)

Mean Opportunity Cost
Minus Real Cost Estimate

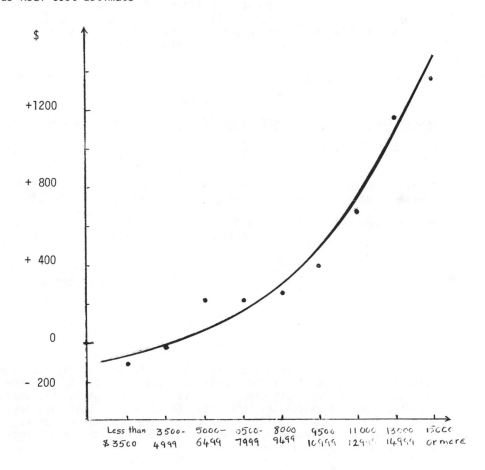

Full Family Income

with institutional constraints in their time allocation then aggregate
output could be increased through voluntary reallocation of resources.
The argument assumes, however, that non-pecuniary rewards (e.g., task
variety) are distributed evenly between market and non-market
productive activities. [17]

TABLE 4-8

MEAN DIFFERENCES BETWEEN OPPORTUNITY COST AND MARKET
PRICE ESTIMATES OF THE VALUE OF HOUSEWORK
AND HOME PRODUCTION WITHIN AGE
AND EDUCATIONAL GROUPS,
1964
(For 1803 families whose heads were not retired or not
housewives 55 or older)

Education	Age		
	Less than 35	35 - 64	65 or older
Less than 12 grades	63* (300)	222 (99)	181 (285)
12 grades but no college degree	882 (230)	605 (120)	818 (499)
College degree	937 (355)	790 (310)	873 (901)

* Standard errors are given in parentheses below the means.

---

[17]
Market prices are averages that tend to over estimate the
value of non-market output for people with low productivity and under
estimate it for those with high productivity. Although in this study,
market prices are calculated separately for different tasks and are
adjusted for state price differences their "average" nature raises doubt
to whether they reflect the real value of non-market output as compared
to opportunity cost estimates.

4.2.2 Volunteer work

The average value of volunteer work is estimated at $204.[18]
Our findings show, as do other studies, that there is a positive
relation between the value of volunteer work and disposable income
(Figure 4-6).[19] Also, we find that, as expected, the value of volunteer
work for married people ($227) is greater than for single people
especially for single women ($139) and that the young uneducated have
the lowest value of such income ($71).

4.2.3 Education

In 1964, the value of time spent by heads of families on
education was $141.[20] About 17 percent of heads of families took some
courses or lessons. Our estimate is based on an investment approach
to human resources. The individual will use his time resource in taking
courses and studying until the present value product of his time
invested, is equal to its present cost which is equal to his net hourly
earnings. There are many other costs and considerations involved in
the decision to take further education, or more generally to invest in
human capital.[21] But given such decision, the allocation of time will
be governed by the present earning potential. Younger people are

---

[18] Our estimate is lower than the $260 estimate reported by
J. Morgan, I. Sirageldin and N. Baerwaldt, Productive Americans, p. 140.
Since the latter multiplied an unadjusted average hourly earnings of heads
of families ($3.07) by the reported hours of volunteer work done by heads
or by wives. In this study, hourly earnings of heads and of wives adjusted
for disequilibrium situations, were used on individual basis to calculate
the value of volunteer work.

[19]
[20] Morgan et. al., Income and Welfare in the United States, pp. 257-287.

For an analysis of the hours spent on education by those heads
of families, see J. Morgan, I. Sirageldin, and N. Baerwaldt, Productive
Americans, pp. 154-157.

[21] Gary S. Becker, Human Capital, (New York: National Bureau of
Economic Research, 1964), pp. 49-66.

FIGURE 4-6

VALUE OF VOLUNTEER WORK BY THE LOG OF
DISPOSABLE INCOME - 1964
(For all 2214 families)

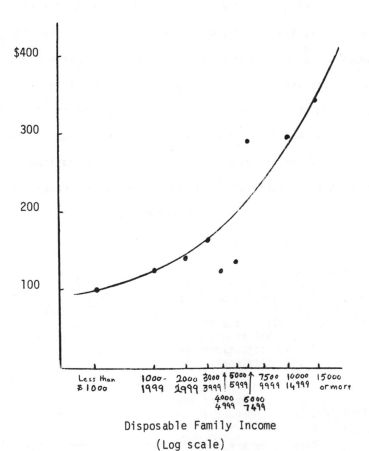

Value of Volunteer Work

Disposable Family Income

(Log scale)

expected to devote more time to education since their opportunity cost is low (low present hourly earnings) and also they expect to collect the returns over more years. On the other hand, people with expected short pay out periods (e.g. graduate students) will also devote more of their resources to such investment.

Table 4-9 illustrates those propositions: within the same educational groups, those under 35 have the larger means, (i.e., will collect returns over more years), and within the same age groups, those with higher levels of education have larger means (expected short payout periods). This general relationship holds true even if we excluded full time students. We notice, however, that one reason for the higher values of time spent on education by those with higher levels of education is their higher wages (opportunity costs). In 1964, 9 percent of those heads of families who took courses or lessons were full time students and the average value of their time devoted to education was $4827.[22]

4.2.4   Car services

Cars represent an important fraction of the American family's purchases of durables. An attempt has been made in this study to estimate the value of income received from car services. In 1964, car income was about $44 per family and car consumption $197 (or $2.1 and 9.3 billions for all U.S. Families). Car income is taken simply as 6

_____

[22] Our estimates of the value of time devoted to education refers only to heads of families but not to other adults in the family. This is indeed a small part of total adult time devoted to education. A global estimate of the value of adult time devoted to education is useful in assessing the full cost of education as an investment activity especially in developing nations. In a recent paper, D. Seers and R. Jolly argue that educational expenditures should be treated as a form of capital formation in national accounting, "The Treatment of Education in National Accounting," Income and Wealth, 3,(September,1966) 195-209. We argue that the value of adult studying time should be included as well.

TABLE 4-9

THE VALUE OF TIME DEVOTED TO EDUCATION WITHIN
AGE AND EDUCATIONAL GROUPS, 1964

	Age		
Education	Less than 35	35 - 64	65 or older
Less than 12 grades	$47[*] (45)	$16 (8)	$15 (40)
12 grades but no college degree	620 (180)	59 (30)	13 (18)
College degree	711 (240)	188 (140)	23[**] (40)

[*] Standard errors are given in parentheses under the means
[**] Fewer than 50 cases.

percent of the depreciated value of the car (i.e., the interest that
could have been earned by investing the value of the net worth of the
car(s). Car depreciation is estimated at a rate of 25 percent per annum
with a floor of 2 percent of the original price to approximate scrap
values.[23] Income from second cars is estimated at two-thirds of that
of the first car, and from other extra cars at one-third. Car consumption is defined to equal the estimated car income plus depreciation.[24]

Car services are used as inputs either in the family's
productive activities or in its consumptive and leisure activities.[25]

---

[23] See H.S. Houthakker and J. Haldi, Household Investment in
Automobiles, (Palo Alto: Department of Economics, Stanford University,
1957), Table I.

[24] The age and model of the first car and the number of cars owned
by the family were readily available on the analysis tape, but not their
market prices. Cars were classified into three categories: low, medium,
and high priced cars with average prices $2,000, $3,000, and $4,000
respectively. Depreciated car values were then calculated using the
following formula:

$P_i (1-.25)^t$ where P_i = car price, and t = car age; i = 1,2,3
Thus, for a family owning a two-year old Cadillac:

Depreciated value = .75 x .75 x 4000 = $2,250
Car income = .06 x 2,250 = $135
Car consumption = (.75 x .25 x 4,000) + 135 = $885

A more reliable procedure, would have used information from
The National Auto Dealers Association to estimate the car values given
its make and model year. However, our procedure is both simple and
reasonable.

[25] The purpose of this section is to examine car income within
various population groups. The intention, however, is not to develop
a complex model, but rather to examine the conformity of our estimates
with expected behavior.

The interaction of those two types of decisions, along with the fact that car income is a product of both quality and quantity of cars owned by the family, results in a complex pattern which is related simultaneously to the marital status, age, number of earners, family size, education, and income of the family unit.[26]

Our data show that single people, especially women, have less car income than married people, and that car income increases systematically with the number of major earners in the family. Those variables are clearly related to disposable income and the latter has a systematic and positive effect on car income (Figure 4-7). Average car income varied between $5 for families with less than $1,000 disposable incomes (most of which have no cars) to $112 for families with incomes of $15,000 or more.

To gain a better understanding of the complex interactions among the various factors that influence car income, value of car income for married people is tabulated according to age and education of the family head (Table 4-10). Within any given educational group, middle aged people have the largest car income since they have larger families with relatively more earners.[27] On the other hand, car income increases systematically with education within any given age group. However, the extent of increase in car income diminishes as age increases. One

---

[26] See for example Marvin Snowbarger and D.B. Suits, "Consumer Expenditures for Durable Goods", in Determinants of Investment Behavior, (New York: National Bureau of Economic Research, 1967), pp. 346-355. Also, Martin H. David, Family Composition, pp. 82-93; Fredrick May, The Use of Consumer Survey Data in Forcasts of Domestic Demand for Consumer Durable Goods (Unpublished Ph.D Thesis) Ann Arbor, The University of Michigan, 1958.

[27] This is not in full agreement with May's finding that consumption of cars declines as the age of the head of the spending unit increases. ibid, p. 174. The age effect is clearly non-linear.

FIGURE 4-7

CAR INCOME BY DISPOSABLE INCOME
(For all 2214 families)

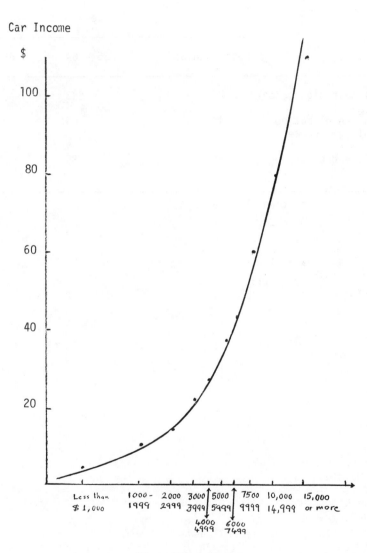

Disposable Income
(Log Scale)

TABLE 4-10

CAR INCOME WITHIN AGE AND EDUCATIONAL GROUPS
(For all 1640 married people)

	Age		
Education	Less than 35	35 - 64	65 or older
Less than high school	$25	$43	$28
High school but no college degree	44	66	40
College degree	64	86	46*

* Fewer than 25 cases

$F_c = 25.6$

$F_{.01} = 2.9$

$R^2 = .13$

explanation is that the demand of the more educated (richer) older

couples for car services is mostly for consumptive activities (improved

quality but not quantity), while that of the more educated (richer)

young couples is both for better quality and more quantity because of

extra earners in the family.

4.3   Potential Family Income

Potential income gives the level of family income that could be

achieved if every earner in the family is satisfied with the allocation

of his time between work and leisure.[28] In this study, we calculate

---

[28] Our definition of potential income differs from that of
potential aggregate output employed recently in the economic literature.
The latter is usually defined as:
> "that level of Gross National Product which the economy
> could produce at a given time under conditions of
> reasonably full employment of the labor force and
> normal utilization of plant capacity "

Charles L. Schultze, National Income Analysis, (New Jersey: Prentice-
Hall Inc., 1964), p. 111.
Many recent studies addressed itself to the empirical measure-
ment of potential aggregate output in terms of some criterion of
"reasonable" full employment (e.g., 96% of the labor force) and of "normal"
utilization of plant capacity. See for example, Locke Anderson and Jarvis
Babcock, "Measuring Potential Gross National Product," paper delivered
December 1964 at the Meeting of the Econometric Society; Edwin Kuh,
"Measurement of Potential Output", American Economic Review, September
1966, Vol. LVI, 758-776; A. Okun, "Potential GNP: Its Measurement and
Significance," American Statistical Association, Proceedings, 1962,
98-104; J.W. Knowles and C.B. Warden, Jr., "The Potential Economic Growth
in the United States", Study Paper No. 20, prepared for the Joint Economic
Committee in connection with the study Employment Growth and Price Levels,
86th Cong., 2nd Sess., Washington 1960; and Economic Report of the President,
January 1967, pp. 42-45.
Although some attention has been given to the fact that the impact
and distribution of "reasonable" unemployment rates are usually "un-reason-
able" for some groups of the population, no attempt has been made to estimate
and examine the value of the resultant loss in families' income. Our
concept of potential income is more general and humane. It stems from a
recent contribution to the analysis of families' unwanted leisure, J. Morgan,
I. Sirageldin, and N. Baerwaldt, Productive Americans, pp. 90-100.

potential family income by adding to full income an estimate of the
extent of disequilibrium in families' time allocation, namely, the time
lost because of sickness or unemployment, and the value of desired
more (add) or fewer (subtract) hours of work. The gap between actual
and potential income gives a measure of the value of families' unwanted
leisure which is also an estimate of peoples' reservior of potential
output.

In 1964, the average gap between actual and potential family
income was $592. Of course, it was those in the blue-collar and
clerical and sales occupations whose actual income was far below its
potential since their incidence and duration of their unemployment
experience is greater than the average (Figure 4-8).   Formal education
distinguishes even more clearly than occupation between those who have
much and little unwanted leisure. Excluding those who were retired in
1964, the dramatic association between lack of formal education and
unwanted leisure within age groups is shown in Table 4-11. The value
of unwanted leisure is greatest among uneducated people regardless of
their age, while the youngest people suffered the most from their lack
of education (the gap was 20 percent of disposable income for the uneducated young).[29]

Our measure of unwanted leisure includes three components that
might have offsetting effects on the final value of the measure. And
although it is the combined effects of those components that best indicate
the family's potential (e.g., the incidence of sickness increases with age
but sick people would prefer less work) we shall examine separately and
briefly the value of time lost because of sickness or unemployment and the

---

[29]This age-education effect is similar to that reported in
Productive Americans although the dependent variables in the two studies
differ substantially, ibid., 96.

FIGURE 4-8

THE GAP BETWEEN ACTUAL AND POTENTIAL
INCOME WITHIN OCCUPATIONAL GROUPS

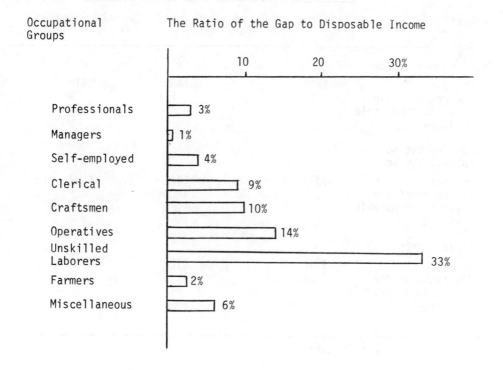

Occupational Groups

The Ratio of the Gap to Disposable Income

TABLE 4-11

THE GAP BETWEEN ACTUAL AND POTENTIAL INCOME
WITHIN AGE AND EDUCATIONAL GROUPS
(For 1803 families: not retired heads of families or not housewives
55 or older)

| | Age | | |
Education	Less than 35	35 - 64	65 or older
Less than 12 grades			
The gap	$939	$880	$615
The ratio of the gap to disposable income	20%	13%	9%
12 grades but no college degree			
The gap	$377	$447	$ 64
The ratio of the gap to disposable income	6%	5%	*
College degree			
The gap	$ 57	$128	$ 41
The ratio of the gap to disposable income	1%	1%	*

* Fewer than 50 cases.

value of desired more or less work since each has its special interest.

4.3.1   The value of time lost because of unemployment or sickness

This value has been estimated by multiplying hours of sickness
or unemployment reported by heads of families or their wives by their
respective hourly earnings.[30]   Ideally, one would like to separate
unemployment from sickness since they are basically different constraints
that have different effects on people's desires for work and that
require different policy measures.[31]   Table 4-12 shows that the mean
values of unemployment and sickness were $534 for those who would like
more work and $476 for those who would like less work.   This smaller
than expected difference suggests that the desire for less work might
be a result of deteriorated health (many of this latter group were
relatively old).

----

[30] The actual question asked to elicit information about hours
of sickness or unemployment was:

> "How many weeks were there last year when you
> weren't working because of illness or unemployment?
> On the average, about how many hours a week did you
> work when you were working?"

[31] There was no physical way to separate sickness from
unemployment since only their total was recorded in the interview.

TABLE 4-12

VALUE OF UNEMPLOYMENT OR SICKNESS BY
DESIRE FOR MORE OR LESS WORK
(For 1636 families who were in labor force in early 1965)

| | Mean Value of Unemployment or Sickness | |
	Mean*	Number of Cases
Desire more work	$534 (97)	569
Satisfied	$397 (76)	849
Desire less work	$476 (132)	218
All Families	$455 (55)	1636

*Standard errors of the mean are given in paranetheses under
the means.

4.3.2   The value of desired more or fewer hours of work

On balance, heads of American families would like to work
$93 worth of extra hours.[32] However, the average value of extra work
for those who would like more work was $460 and for those who would
prefer to work fewer hours was -$629. This means that although, on
balance, the contribution to national output was less than $100 per
family, the underlying reallocation of resources that would have brought
it about is enormous. One should not underestimate the extent of disequilibrium in the society nor the cost of correcting it.

Expressed desires for more or less work, for a given wage rate,
is an indication of disequilibrium in the leisure-work-time allocation.

---

[3] The following question was asked for heads of families who
were in the labor force when interviewed:

> "Some people would like to work more hours a week if
> they could be paid for it. Others would prefer to
> work fewer hours a week even if they earned less.
> How do you feel about this?"

Given the people's response to that question and given their reported
hourly earnings, the following procedure was used to estimate the
value of their desired more or less work:

Type of Response	Multiply Reported Hours of Work by:
Strongly prefer more work	.10
Prefer more work	.05
Satisfied or don't know	0
Prefer less work	-.05
Strongly prefer less work	-.10

For example, the value of desired work for a man who strongly preferred
more work and who has reported 1,000 hours of work for money is equal to:

1000 x .10 x adjusted hourly earnings (i.e., adjusted for
sickness and unemployment as indicated in Table 2-3).

Existing institutions require a fixed amount of weekly hours of work
for most of the working class (i.e., an "all or none" type of arrange-
ment). Accordingly, we would expect that within a given educational
group, older people prefer less work since they have both relatively
higher pay and declining health. And within a given age group, the
more educated prefer less work since they would be willing to buy
some leisure time back if they could. Table 4-13 illustrates these
points: the uneducated young would like to work the most both because
of his low pay and the frequency of his unemployment; while the
educated old would like to work the least both because of his high pay
and his health.

Finally, to verify further the hypothesis that some of the high
income groups work more hours than they would actually like to,[33] the
value of desired more work is tabulated according to occupation.
(Table 4-14). The only two groups that have negative means on their
desired extra work are the managers and officials and the self-employed
businessmen who are probably pressured by a demanding business.

---

[33] See, Morgan et. al., Income and Welfare in the United States,
p. 326.

TABLE 4-13

AVERAGE VALUE OF DESIRED MORE OR FEWER HOURS
WITHIN AGE AND EDUCATIONAL GROUPS
(For all 1639 heads of families who were working in early 1965)

	Age		
Education	Less than 35	35 - 64	65 or older
Less than 12 grades			
Value of desired work	$298	$130	$ -21
Percent who like more work minus who like less	55%	28%	5%
12 Grades, no college degree			
Value of desired work	$269	$ 63	$ -19*
Percent who like more work minus who like less	50%	16%	- 4%
College Degree			
Value of desired work	$171	$ -5	$-100*
Percent who like more work minus who like less	9%	11%	- 7%

* Fewer than 50 cases.

TABLE 4-14

AVERAGE VALUE OF DESIRED MORE OR
FEWER HOURS BY OCCUPATION

Occupation	Average Value of Desired Work	Percent who Desire more work minus who desire less
	$	%
Professionals	57	12
Managers	-74	- 4
Self-employed Business	-16	0
Clerical	180	27
Craftsman	125	25
Operatives	230	42
Unskilled	172	33
Farmers	45	12
Miscellaneous	132	40

CHAPTER 5

THE DISTRIBUTION OF WELFARE

A New York lady, for instance, having a nature of
exquisite sensibility, orders an elegant rosewood
and silver coffin, upholstered in pink satin, for
her dead dog. It is made: and meanwhile a live
child is prowling barefooted and hunger-stunned
in the frozen gutter outside.[1]

5.0   Introduction

The validity of any study of income distribution depends on

at least five factors: (1) the concept of family income adopted;

(2) the definition of income expenditure unit used; (3) the length

of time over which the income flow is measured; (4) the measure of

income distribution employed; and (5) statistical errors resulting

mainly from sampling variability, non-reporting, and errors of response.

Statistical errors have been discussed in Chapter 3 and a brief

discussion of some measures of inequality has been presented in

Chapter 4.

The first three issues are more basic to the central theme of

this study since the interest is not in presenting exact measurements

of income inequality but rather in developing income measures that

would better reflect the real welfare of American families. Various

measures of income and welfare are compared and evaluated in the following

section. The last section presents the empirical findings in an attempt

to explain differences in the real welfare of American families.

---

[1] Bernard Shaw, Fabian Essays, (London, 1950), p. 24.

5.1   Measures of Welfare

In previous chapters we developed the concept of "full income",
which can be thought of as income earned by the family's labor and
capital. It represents the degree of control over total economic
resources that the family has. Full income is clearly superior to
money income as a measure of families' welfare. However, we argue that
it has some serious deficiencies. Welfare is essentially a relation
between means and wants. The distribution of full income does not
reflect the distribution of real welfare since wants or needs differ
among families with different sizes, ages, or education. In other words,
all our adjustments and imputations will not improve much the power of
full income as a measure of real welfare unless some account is made
for differences in family structure. Furthermore, real welfare will
depend on how many hours of leisure the family has to give up in order
to earn its current full income.

5.1.1   Adjustments for family needs

The budget needs of each family unit in the sample are estimated
according to data derived from a schedule prepared in 1959 by the
Community Council of Greater New York.[2] The schedule allows for variations
in the maintenance needs of families with different structure. Costs are

---

[2] This is the same procedure used by J. Morgan et.al., Income and
Welfare in the United States, p. 188. For a discussion of these measures,
see Martin David, "Welfare, Income, and Budget Needs," The Review of
Economics and Statistics, XLI (November, 1959), pp. 393-399.

deflated by the cost of living index (108) and the cost of housing (107.2)
in order to update the schedule. Table 5-1 gives the estimated basic
needs in 1959 and 1964 prices. An estimate of the budget requirements
of each family is prepared by adding the various dollar estimates of the
basic needs for each member in the family. An equivalent adult unit
measure (EQV.) that allows for variation in the size and composition of
each family is calculated based on the same schedule (Table 5-1). That
measure is highly related to family size (Figure 5-1), and is used to
calculate per equivalent adult income measures. Income per equivalent
adults could be used as a better estimate of the level of welfare
enjoyed by each unit; this measure is referred to as the EQV. measure.[3]

5.1.2   Adjustment for leisure time

Measures of income, whether adjusted or unadjusted for family
structure,do not take account of the fact that income is a product of
hourly earnings and hours spent working. They assume that income is
the only dimension of welfare and that people's indifference curves
between income and leisure form straight lines parallel to the time
axis (i.e., the marginal utility of leisure is always zero). Two families
with the same income are assumed to have the same level of welfare even
if one of them spent half its time earning that income. It is clear
that the level of welfare enjoyed by the family cannot be measured without
taking account of the time spent by the family in earning its income.

---

[3] Morgan et. al., took the ratio of gross disposable income to
the estimated budget requirements as an estimate of the level of families'
welfare, Income and Welfare in the United States, pp. 189-190. As will
be apparent in the next section, this measure lacks a time dimension.

TABLE 5-1

SCHEDULE OF ESTIMATED ANNUAL COSTS OF GOODS AND SERVICES

	1959	1964	EQV.*
I. Food, clothing, and other personal costs			
Head			
In labor force	$1,144	$1,238	1.00
Not in labor force	676	730	.79
Wife			
In labor force	1,092	1,180	.57
Not in labor force	546	590	.32
Other adults			
In labor force	1,196	1,290	.62
Not in labor force	546	590	.32
Children	494	535	.30
II. Rent, utilities, and other costs			
1 person family unit	1,040	1,125	
2 persons	1,248	1,350	
3 persons	1,404	1,520	
4 persons	1,508	1,630	
5 persons	1,664	1,800	
6 persons	1,924	2,070	
7 persons	2,080	2,242	
8 persons or more	2,184	2,362	

*Equivalent adult units (e.g. .78=[730+1,125] ÷ [1,238+1,125];

.57 =[1,180+117] ÷ [1,238+1,125],where $177=the average additional housing requrement per person. In actual analysis, however, the exact additional housing requirement has been calculated.

Source: Adapted from the Community Council of Greater New York, Budget Standard Service, Annual Price Survey and Family Budget Costs, October, 1959. Also cited in Morgan et.al., Income and Welfare, p. 189.

FIGURE 5-1

MEAN EQV ADULT MEASURE BY
NUMBER OF PEOPLE IN THE FAMILY

Mean EQV Adult Unit

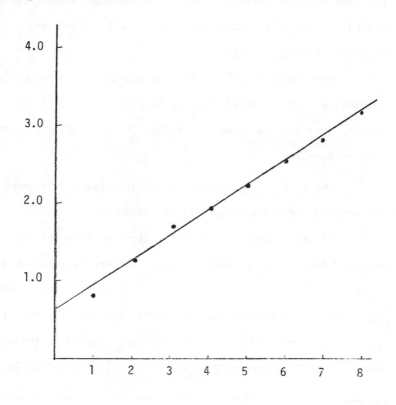

Number of People (in the family)

Our estimate of family's welfare will be based on the following relation:

(1) $\quad W_{it} \quad = I \ (EQV) \ \times \ L_t$

where $\quad W_{it} \quad$ = welfare per unit of time for the ith family

$\quad I(EQV)$ = per equivalent adult unit income

$\quad L_t \quad$ = leisure time available for heads of families and their wives per unit of non-sleeping time (i.e., 16 hours per day per person).[4]

Thus, two families with similar incomes and needs will not have the same value of welfare if their time devoted to work was not the same. Indeed, the one with fewer hours of work will be better off (i.e., will have more leisure to enjoy).

Relation (1) implies that the isoquants showing welfare-equivalent combinations of income and leisure have unitary elasticity. This becomes more apparent when we rewrite relation (1) in terms of income as follows:

(2) $\quad I_i \ (EQV) \ = \ \overline{W}_{it} \ \times \ L_{it}^{-1}$

where W_{it} = a constant level of welfare. Figure 5-2 illustrates the assumed indifference map between income and leisure.

If our assumptions about families' welfare reflect actual behavior, we would expect that people with lower welfare measures at a given income prefer more work, and for a given level of welfare the higher the income the lower the preference for more work. This pattern is evident when data on per equivalent adult full incomes are tabulated by the welfare measure and the desire to work more or fewer hours (Table 5-2). The numbers in

---

[4] Leisure time is taken as a residual by subtracting for each person the time spent on his (her) various productive activities from 16 hours. For those who were sick or unemployed, it is assumed that the unwanted leisure was equally divided between productive and leisure activities. Accordingly, only half of reported unwanted leisure is added to leisure (i.e. the LL and HH curves of Figure 2-1 of Chapter 2 have the same slopes at each level of hourly earnings).

FIGURE 5-2

INCOME, LEISURE, AND
WELFARE CONTOURS

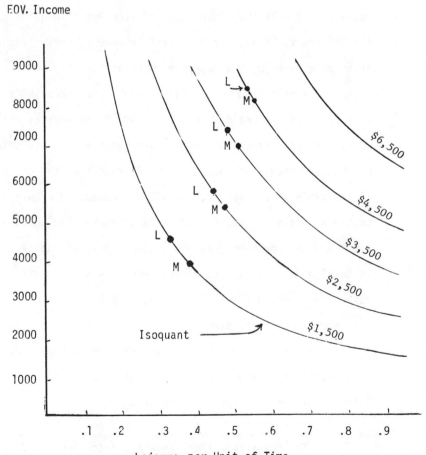

EOV. Income

Leisure per Unit of Time
(The day = 16 hours: 8 hours for maintenance)

the body of the table measure command over goods and services (i.e., average EQV. full incomes), while the classification into rows measures welfare levels to include leisure (i.e., each row represents an indifference curve in Figure 5-3). Thus, at any level of welfare, that is along any row in the table, people with lower full incomes, who also have more but evidently unwanted leisure, desire more work. This finding gives a strong support for the notion that enjoyment of leisure requires not only the consumption of time but also goods and services. People seem to be willing to sacrifice some of their leisure in order to be able to enjoy the remainder more efficiently.

The main findings of Table 5-2 is presented in Figure 5-2 where L represents desires for less work and M represents desires for more work.[5] Average values of welfare are taken at the mid point of each bracket and equivalent adult income is read from the corresponding cell in the table. For example, the $2500 isoquant in Figure 5-2 corresponds to the mid point of the second welfare bracket ($2000-2999) in the Table and the corresponding EQV income for those who desire more work is $5442 and for those who desire less work $5741. Along any indifference curve, for a given level of welfare, people with more leisure desire more work even at the same pay: clearly, they are not in equilibrium.

In the following section we shall examine more closely the distribution of welfare and the allocation of time between work and leisure for various population groups.

---

[5] The transition from Table 5-2 into Figure 5-3 is possible since welfare measure is a product of full income and leisure ratio.

TABLE 5-2

EQV FULL INCOME BY THE DESIRE FOR MORE OR LESS WORK
AND EQV FULL INCOME WELFARE MEASURE
(For all 2214 families)

Desire for More or Less Work

Welfare Measure	All	More	Satisfied	Less	Not Working	Number Cases
	$	$	$	$	$	
Less than 2000	4393	4015	4783	4731	4263	551
2000 - 2999	5504	5442	5918	5741	4651	601
3000 - 3999	6799	7092	7264	7414	5277	444
4000 - 4999	8095	8500	8524	8559	7173	261
5000 or more	16512	11747*	13840	33664*	16063	357
All Families	7567	5830	7550	10733	8110	2214

* Fewer than 50 cases

5.2   The Distribution of Welfare in the U.S.A.

In 1964, the average value of families' welfare measure
was $4,113, that of equivalent adult full income was $7,567, and that
of full income $12,041. These figures indicate that the average per
equivalent adult family size was 1.6 and that families spent about 44
percent of their non-sleeping time on their productive activities. The
'welfare measure' will be lower the higher the family's needs relative
to its full income or the fewer the leisure hours available for its
enjoyment relative to its total time.

There are instances, however, as for example for the elderly
and the retired where measurement of welfare here used is inadequate.
The needs of retired Americans, as measured by the cost schedule in
Table 5-1, are lower than the average by 32 percent while their leisure
time is 12 percent higher. As a result, their average welfare measure
is $6,424, or 56 percent higher than the average. Another factor that
contributes to that calculated higher welfare is their imputed net
rents. Many of the elderly own relatively large homes whose mortgages
are usually paid. Their imputed rents are large but one doubts that
they make full use of large homes.[6] Could we conclude that the welfare
position of the retired is better than the rest of the population?
Probably not. Excessive leisure is of no value to those who cannot
enjoy it because of deteriorating health or lack of the goods and
services that are needed for the consumption of leisure. Adam could

---

[6] By use of homes we mean the   use of housing facilities and
not the depreciation of the house. For a discussion of the housing status
of the aged as well as other problems, see, James Morgan, "Measuring the
Economic Status of the Aged", Age with the Future, (Copenhagen:
Munksgaard, 1964), pp. 492-506.

consume his leisure by simply retiring with Eve under an apple tree, but to enjoy leisure at Miami Beach requires goods and services as well as excess time. We cannot conclude that the retired are better or worse off given our measure, but we can conclude that they ought to be treated separately. In the rest of this chapter we shall exclude from the analysis the families whose heads are either retired or are housewives fifty-five or older.[7]

The distribution of welfare for the 1803 families with non-retired heads is presented in Table 5-3. The lower 25 percent control 10 percent of total welfare while the top 25 percent control 44 percent, as compared to 6 and 52 percent for money income, 10 and 48 percent for equivalent adult disposable income, and 10 and 46 percent for equivalent adult full income. The inclusion of leisure seems to reduce inequality even after allowing for family needs and non-market production. This is also suggested by the low ratio of mean to median (Table 5-3).

Table 5-4 indicates that there is a tendency for people with higher levels of welfare to work more hours (i.e. to have less leisure). This overall pattern might explain some of the apparent low inequality in the distribution of welfare. It cannot be taken, however, as a general tendency that prevails for various subgroups of the population, as is suggested in previous studies.[8] The opposite pattern seems to be the case for major subgroups of the population as will be evident from the following discussion.

---

[7] Our decision to exclude the retired from our discussion does not imply that the incidence of poverty is low among them. On the contrary, many studies indicate that the distribution of the income of the aged is very skewed, ibid., 493. The size of the present sample, however, does not permit an elaborate analysis.

[8] See for example, T. Paul Schultz, The Distribution of Personal Income, p. 38, and James Morgan and others, Income and Welfare in the United States, p. 327, ch. 21.

TABLE 5-3

THE DISTRIBUTION OF WELFARE MEASURE
(For 1803 families whose heads are not
retired or housewives 55 or older)

Welfare Bracket	Percent of Cases	Mean Welfare	Percent of Welfare
	%	$	%
Less than $1500	14	1101	4
1500 - 1999	13	1952	7
2000 - 2499	15	2476	11
2500 - 2999	14	2910	12
3000 - 3499	11	3448	11
3500 - 3999	9	3873	9
4000 - 4499	6	4517	8
4500 - 4999	4	4863	6
5000 - 6999	8	5987	14
7000 or more	4	18004	18
All	100	3586	100

Overall Median	$3280
Ratio of Mean to Median	1.09

TABLE 5-4

WELFARE MEASURE, EQV. FULL INCOME, AND LEISURE
(For 1803 families whose heads are not retired,
or housewives 55 or older)

Bracket EQV Full Income	Mean EQV Full Income	Mean Welfare Measure	Mean Leisure Ratio
	$	$	%
Less than $1500	1015	670	66
1500 - 1999	1813	1226	68
2000 - 2499	2267	1436	63
2500 - 2999	2764	1726	62
3000 - 3499	3250	1949	60
3500 - 3999	3762	2174	58
4000 - 4499	4266	2443	57
4500 - 4999	4745	2603	55
5000 - 6999	5965	3114	52
7000 or more	12043	6522	54

5.3   Families' Welfare Among Population Groups

Except at the two extremes, money income seems to show no relation to the level of welfare enjoyed by the family. The simple correlation is 0.22 between money income and full income, but only 0.09 between money income and the welfare measure.[9] This is an expected tendency, since the measure of welfare accounts for the amount of time devoted to earning the income.

Formal education seems to be an important determinant of welfare. It reflects the family's earning potential as well as its attitudes and motivations that results in better planning and more accumulation. But even within the same education groups, the rank and wealth differ substantially from one age group to the next. One would expect that within education groups, welfare would increase with age, since past accumulation and experience tend to increase total income faster than family size or hours of work. Likewise, within age groups welfare increases with formal education since education has a substantial impact on earnings. Table 5-5 illustrates this pattern. For the least educated people, welfare increased from $1927 for young people to $3694 for working people sixty-five or older. The latter groups has 25 percent more leisure. For young people, the welfare of those with college degrees was more than double of those without high school education. The poorly educated have both less income and less leisure than the well educated.

---

[9] Brackets on money income were used as numbers to calculate these correlations. This, of course, prevents extreme cases from having much influence on the correlation.

TABLE 5-5

MEAN WELFARE MEASURE, EOV. FULL INCOME, AND
LEISURE RATIO BY AGE AND EDUCATION
(For 1803 families whose heads are non-retired
or housewives 55 or older)

	Age		
Education	Less than 35	35 - 64	65 or older
Less than 12 grades			
Welfare measure	$1927	$2931	$3694
Leisure ratio	.43	.48	.54
12 grades, no degree			
Welfare measure	$2881	$3600	$3974[*]
Leisure ratio	.47	.47	.53
College degree			
Welfare measure	$3901	$8401	$10552[*]
Leisure ratio	.51	.54	.60

[*] Fewer than 50 cases

The size of the family is another constraining factor that affects the family's welfare measure. Larger families have a lower welfare measure than smaller families partly because of their larger needs relative to their income and partly they must sacrifice more of their leisure to meet their needs. This pattern is illustrated in Figure 5-3. The leisure ratio is measured on the horizontal axis, EQV. full income is measured on the vertical axis, and welfare indifference curves are assumed but not drawn. The relation between family size and the mean welfare measure is presented in Figure 5-3 where P_i represents a given family size. There is a strong tendency for smaller families to be located towards the North-east direction (i.e.,both higher income and higher leisure). The implication is that larger families will have a lower welfare measure than smaller families regardless of the assumed shape of the welfare function (in the range of common sense).[10]

There are many factors that might be related to families' welfare measure, some are background and constraining factors (e.g. age and education, race, number of people, occupation, owns a business or farm, whether grew up on farm, and present location). Others are motivational(e.g.,N-Achievement index, the frequency of using new things, religious preference). Those variables have been used in a dummy variable regression analysis in an attempt to examine the net

---

[10]Our measure is indeed restricted by its behavioral assumption about the unitary isoquant elasticity between income and leisure. However, it is more realistic than the conventional income-welfare analysis that assumes no value for leisure.

FIGURE 5-3

THE DISTRIBUTION OF WELFARE
AMONG POPULATION GROUPS

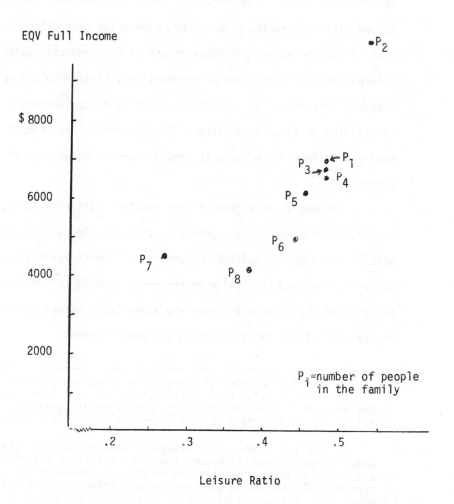

P_i = number of people in the family

effect of each variable. The analysis is restricted to 1549 non-farm families whose heads were in the labor force.

Table 5-6 provides a list of the sets of explanatory variables used in the multivariate analysis, together with the beta coefficient as a measure of importance in reducing predictive error. Tables 5-7 through 5-12 show the detailed subgroup averages and the adjusted subgroup averages.[11] The effect of large families and that of age and education prevails, as expected, even after controlling on the rest of the variables. An index of use of new products representing progressive attitudes seems to be positively related to the welfare measure. The effect of occupation virtually disappears after controlling on age and education. The substantial adjustment for self-employed businessmen presumably result from taking account of owning a business.[12]

Growing up on a farm affects peoples' attitudes and future opportunities since it is probably related to a low quality of education. The adjusted welfare measure is the lowest for those who grew up on the farm and are living in the rural deep South. Neither race nor whether the wife worked have any appreciable effect on families' measure of welfare after adjusting for other factors.

---

[11] For a discussion of dummy variable regression with a special reference to the program used in this analysis, see, Frank Andrews, J. Morgan, and J. Sonquist, Multiple Classification Analysis, (Ann Arbor: Institute for Social Research, 1967) The University of Michigan.

[12] Capital income is a related explanatory variable that was not included in the regression since it was not readily available on the analysis tape. A future analysis that include capital income would be very useful in examining the nature of the substitution between non-earned income and leisure. Such analysis is of special interest to the recent controversy concerning "minimum income".

TABLE 5-6

CHARACTERISTICS USED TO EXPLAIN WELFARE
FAMILY MEASURE IN 1964
(For 1549 non-farm families whose heads
were in the labor force)

Characteristic	Relative Importance
Number of people in the family	.078
Age and education	.075
Use of new products	.049
Whether owns a business	.016
Occupation	.015
Farm background and present location	.010
Whether wife worked	.008
Religious preference	.001
Race	.000

R^2 = .36

$\overline{Y}$ = $3363

TABLE 5-7

WELFARE MEASURE IN 1964: DEVIATIONS
FOR NUMBER OF PEOPLE

Number of People	Number of Families	Percent of Families	Unadjusted Deviation	Adjusted Deviation
	Cases	%	$	$
One person family	176	11.4	-25	148
Two person family	363	23.4	1166	955
Three person family	297	19.2	-7.1	97
Four person family	329	21.2	-79	-195
Five person family	194	12.5	-488	-527
Six person family	94	6.1	-1151	-933
Seven person family	45	2.9	-2222	-1698
Eight or more	51	3.3	-1724	-1390

TABLE 5-8

WELFARE MEASURE IN 1964: DEVIATIONS
FOR AGE AND EDUCATION

Age and Education	Number of Families	Percent of Families	Unadjusted Deviation	Adjusted Deviation
	Cases	%	$	$
Under 35				
0 - 11 grades	112	7.2	-1326	-369
12 grades	222	14.3	-636	-449
College degree	75	4.8	471	62
35 - 64				
0 - 11 grades	516	33.3	-504	-223
12 grades	423	27.3	252	-64
College degree	140	9.0	2270	1659
65 or older				
0 - 11 grades	36	2.3	667	249
12 grades	18	1.2	859	-81
College degree	7	.5	7190	5509

TABLE 5-9

WELFARE MEASURE IN 1964: DEVIATION
FOR USE OF NEW PRODUCTS*

Index Score (Number of items used)	Number of Families	Percent of Families	Unadjusted Deviation	Adjusted Deviation
	Cases	%	$	$
0	132	8.5	-1491	-937
1	238	15.4	- 950	-586
2	319	20.6	- 391	-156
3	325	21.0	- 231	18
4	293	18.9	736	337
5	196	12.7	1211	703
6	46	3.0	2223	1537

* For a definition and discussion of that index, See J. Morgan and others, Productive Americans, pp. 206-233.

TABLE 5-10

WELFARE MEASURE IN 1964: DEVIATION
FOR WHETHER OWN A BUSINESS

Business Ownership	Number of Families	Percent of Families	Unadjusted Deviation	Adjusted Deviation
	Cases	%	$	$
Do not own	1336	86	-184	-122
Owns a business	213	14	1154	762

TABLE 5-11

WELFARE MEASURE IN 1964: DEVIATION
FOR OCCUPATION

Occupation	Number of Families	Percent of Families	Unadjusted Deviation	Adjusted Deviation
Professionals	221	14.3	1079	116
Managers	138	8.9	1340	805
Self-employed business	159	10.3	839	-149
Clerical	217	14.0	-175	-215
Craftsmen	326	21.0	-167	115
Operatives	288	18.6	-783	-138
Unskilled	200	12.9	-1194	-320

TABLE 5-12

WELFARE MEASURE IN 1964: DEVIATION
FOR WHETHER GREW UP ON FARM AND PRESENT LOCATION

	Number of Families	Percent of Families	Unadjusted Deviation	Adjusted Deviation
	Cases	%	$	$
Did not grow up on farm				
Lives in urban not in deep South	685	44.2	417	208
Lives in urban deep South	187	12.1	-311	-245
Lives in rural not deep South	117	7.6	18	-358
Lives in rural deep South	27	1.7	555	541
Grew up on farm				
Lives in urban not in deep South	181	11.7	- 41	- 25
Lives in urban deep South	112	7.2	- 7	50
Lives in rural not deep South	113	7.3	-446	-239
Lives in rural deep South	127	8.2	-1466	-342

CHAPTER 6

SUMMARY AND CONCLUSIONS

" At this point I lay aside my pen: the sequel
of the story may haply commend itself to
another"

Xenophon, _Hellenica_

This study demonstrates the importance and feasability
of measuring non-market income. As a first step some theoretical
discussions were presented which demonstrated that formal economic
theory of the household could logically extend to the analysis of
non-market activities.

The average value of a family's unpaid output was estimated
at almost $4,000 or about 50 percent of disposable income. Ninety
percent of this imputed value was in the form of housework and other
types of home production. The rest was in the form of volunteer work,
time spent on education and income from car services.

The relation of market to non-market output was examined, and
it was found that people with low incomes tend to produce relatively
more non-market goods and services than people with high incomes.
Further, full income, defined to include market and non-market output,
is distributed more equally than money income.

This trade-off between market and non-market activities makes
it evident that the exclusion of non-market income coupled with a
secular shift from non-market to market activities places an upward
bias on the ratio of growth of GNP and makes comparisons over time and

120

across countries highly questionable. Further, cyclical variations in the ratio of market to nonmarket productive activities overstate the true short run variation in real GNP.

The extent of disequilibrium in the labor market, (defined as the value of time lost because of sickness or unemployment and the dissatisfaction with the number of hours of work by heads of families) was estimated at about $ 36 billion dollars in 1964.[1] This gap between actual and potential income was greatest among the uneducated young.

Finally an attempt has been made to define a measure of family welfare that accounts for difference in family structure as well as for the cost of time devoted to productive activities. For any given age, education seemed to have a strong effect on the distribution of welfare and the well educated tend to have more of both leisure and income.

The implication of the analysis to problems of poverty are yet to be developed. The present approach is but a beginning that needs further refinements. A similar analysis for another set of data will make it possible to measure the extent of the shift between market and non-market activities. It will also serve as a check on the reliability of the present estimates.

---

[1] This estimate is calculated by multiplying the value of the gap between potential and actual income (i.e.$592) by 60 million families. See section 4.3 above. Rough estimates of aggregates could be estimated by multiplying the reported overall averages by 60 millions. However, the estimated aggregates are subject to greater errors especially if it is based on a mean for a small subgroup. See, Kish,L.,Survey Sampling, pp.433-436.

BIBLIOGRAPHY

Ackley, Gardner. Macroeconomic Theory, New York: The Macmillan & Co. Ltd. 1961, pp. 55-57.

Aitchison, J., and Brown, J.A.C. The Lognormal Distribution, Cambridge: Cabrdige University Press, 1963, pp. 8-13 and 154-155.

Alker, Hayward R. Jr., and Russel, Bruce. "On measuring Inequality", Behavioral Science, 9, July 1964, pp. 207-218.

Anderson, Locke, and Babcock, Jarvis. "Measuring Potential Gross National Product", Paper delivered December 1964, at the Meeting of the Econometric Society.

Batchelder, Alan B. "Decline in the Relative Income of Negro Men", The Quarterly Journal of Economics, LXXVIII, November, 1966.

Becker, G.S. The Economics of Discrimination, Chicago: University of Chicago Press, 1957.

_____ " The Economics of Education", The Changing American Economy, Edited by John R. Coleman, New York: Basic Books Inc., September 1966.

_____ Human Capital, New York: National Bureau of Economic Research, 1964, pp. 49-66.

_____ "Investment in Human Capital: a theoretical analysis", The Journal of Political Economy, Vol. LXX, No. 5, part 2, pp. 9-49, October 1962.

_____ "A Theory of the Allocation of Time", Economic Journal, LXXXV, September, 1965, pp. 493-517.

Berry, Denstone. "Modern Welfare Analysis and the Forms of Income Distribution", Income Distribution and Social Policy, Edited by Alan T. Peacock, London: The Alden Press, 1954.

Boulding, K." Some Difficulties in the Concept of Economic Output", in Output, and Productivity Measurement,(Princeton:Princeton Univ,1961).

Cairncross, A.K. "Economic Schizophrenia", Scottish Journal of Political Economy, February, 1958.

Cartwright, Dorwin P. "Analysis of Qualitative Material", Research
      Methods in Behavioral Sciences, NewYork: The Drydon Press
      Inc., 1953, pp. 421-470.

Community Council of Greater New York, Budget Study Service. Annual
      Price Survey and Family Budget Costs, October 1959.

David, Martin H. Family Composition and Consumption, Amsterdam:
      North Holland Publishing Co., 1962, p.14.

_____ "Welfare, Income, and Budget Needs", The Review of
      Economics and Statistics, Vol. XLI, November 1959, pp.
      393-399.

Economic Report of The President. January 1967, pp. 42-45

Foote, Nelson N. "The Time Dimension and Consumer Behavior", Joseph
      W. Neuman (ed.) On Knowing the Consumer, New York: John
      Wiley & Sons, 1966, p.39.

Gage, Marie G. "The Work Load and Its Value for 50 Homemaker, Tompkins
      County, New York", (Unpublished Ph.D. Thesis), College of
      Home Economics, Cornell University, 1960.

Hansen, Morris H., Hurwitz, William N., and Madow, William G. Sample
      Survey Methods and Theory, Vol. II. New York: John Wiley
      & Sons, Inc., 1960.

Houthakker, H.S., and Haldi, J. Household Investment in Automobiles,
      Palo Alto: Departmjent of Economics, Stanford University,
      1957, Table I.

Mincer, Jacob. "Labor Force Participation of Married Woman: a study
      of Labor Supply", in Aspects of Labor Economics, Princeton:
      Princeton University Press, 1962, pp. 63-105.

Katona, George. The Mass Consumption Society, New York: McGraw-Hill
      Book Co., 1964.

_____ , Lininger, C.A., and Mueller, E. Survey of Consumer
      Finances, Ann Arbor: Survey Research Center, The University
      of Michigan, 1965, pp. 3-24, and 227-230.

_____ , and Morgan James. "Retired in Prospect and Retrospect",
      Ann Arbor: Survey Research Center, The University of Michigan,
      1967, (Mimeographed).

Kendall, M.G., and Stuart, A. The Advanced Theory of Statistics, Vol. I,
      London: Charles Griffin & Co. Ltd. 1958.

Kish, Leslie. Survey Sampling, New York: John Wiley & Sons Inc.,
1965.

_____, and Hess, Irene. The Survey Research Center's National
Sample of Dwellings, Ann Arbor: Institute for Social
Research, The University of Michigan, 1965.

Knowles, J.W., and Warden, C.B.,Jr. "The Potential Economic Growth in
the United States", Study Paper No. 20, prepared for
the Joint Economic Committee in connection with the
Study Employment Growth and Price Levels, 86th Cong.,
2nd sess., Washington, D.C. 1960.

Korbel, John. " Labor Force Entry and Attachment of Young People",
Journal of the American Statistical Association, Vol.
61, March 1966, pp. 117-127.

Kuh, Edwin. "Measurement of Potential Output", American Economic Review,
September, 1966, Vol. LVI, pp.758-776.

Kuznets, Simon. National Income and Its Composition, 1919-1938, New York:
National Bureau of Economic Research, 1941.

Lancaster, K.J. "A New Approach to Consumer Theory", The Journal of
Political Economy, LXXXIV, April, 1966.

Lasser , J.K. Your Income Tax, New York: Simon and Schuster, 1965,
Tables P21.00, pp. 160-164.

Marsh, John and Stafford, Frank. " Income Foregone: The Effects of
Values on Pecuniary Behavior", National Opinion Research,
University of Chicago, March 1966. (Mimeographed).

Marshall, Alfred. Principles of Economics, 8th edition, London:
Macmillan & Co. Ltd., 1920, pp. 628-631.

May, Fredrick. The Use of Consumer Survey Data in Forecasts of Domestic
Demand for Consumer Durable Goods. Ann Arbor: The University
of Michigan, 1958. (Unpublished Ph.D. Thesis).

Meade, E. M. "The Employment of Married Women," The Three Bank Review,
June 1967, No. 74.

Morgan, James N. " Economic Viewpoint on Family Research",Ann Arbor:Survey
Research Center, The University of Michigan,1966.(Mimeographed).

_____ "Measuring the Economic Status of the Aged", Age with
the Future, Copenhagen: Munksgaard, 1964, pp. 492-506.

_____ " A Review of Recent Research on Consumer Behavior",
Consumer Behavior, Ed. L. Clark, New York: Harper &
Bros., 1958, pp. 92-219.

Morgan, James N. Time, Work, and Welfare,[1] Patterns of Market Behavior, Essays in Honor of Philip Taft, Edited by Michael J. Brennan, 1965.

_____, David , M., Cohen, W., and Brazer, H. Income and Welfare in the United States, New York: McGraw Hill, 1962, pp. 95-105.

_____, Sirageldin, Ismail, and Baerwaldt, Nancy. Productive Americans, Ann Arbor: Survey Research Center, Monograph 43, 1966.

Musgrave, Richard A. The Theory of Public Finance, New York: McGraw Hill, 1955, pp. 232-256.

Okun, A. "Potential GNP: Its Measurement and Significance", American Statistical Association, Proceedings, 1962, pp. 98-104.

Rayack, Elton. "Discrimination and the Occupational Progress of Negroes", Review of Economics and Statistics, XLIII, May 1961, pp. 209-214.

Robinson, Joan. Economic Philosophy, Chicago: Aldine Publishing Co., 1963, p.75.

Robinson, John. The Workday, Ann Arbor: Institute for Social Research, The University of Michigan, 1967.

_____, and Converse, Philip E. 66 Basic Tables on Time - Budget Data for the United States, Monograph, Ann Arbor: Institute for Social Research, The University of Michigan, 1966.

Schultz, T. Paul. The Distribution of Personal Income, Joint Economic Committee, Congress of the United States, 88th. Congress 2nd sess., December 1964, pp. 73-77.

Schultz, Theodore W. "Reflections on Investment in Man", The Journal of Political Economy, Vol. LXX, No.5, Part 2, pp. 1-8, October 1962.

Schultze, Charles L. National Income Analysis, New Jersey: Prentice Hall Inc., 1964, p.111.

Seers, D., and Jolly, R. "The Treatment of Education in National Accounting", Income and Wealth, 3, September, 1966, pp. 195-209.

Sirken, Monroe G., Maynes, E. Scott, and Frechtling, John A. "The Survey of Consumer Finances and the Census Quality Check," in Conference on Research in Income and Wealth, An Appraisal of the 1950 Census Income Data. Vol. 23 of Studies in Income and Wealth, Princeton University Press, 1958, pp. 165-167.

Shaw, Bernard. Fabian Essays, London, 1950, p.24.

Smith, Adam. The Wealth of Nations, New York: The Modern Library, 1937, p.314.

Snedecor, George W. Statistical Methods Applied to Experiments in Agriculture and Biology, 5th edition, Ames: The College Press, 1956, pp. 257-285.

Snowbarger, Marvin, and Suits, D.B. "Consumer Expenditures for Durable Goods", Determinants of Investment Behavior, New York: National Bureau of Economic Research, 1967, pp. 346-355.

Somers, Gerald G. "The Rich, the Poor, and the Others", The Changing American Economy, Edited by John R. Coleman, New York: Basic Books Inc., Publishers, September 1966.

Sonquist, John, and Morgan, James. The Detection of Interaction Effects, Ann Arbor: Survey Research Center, The University of Michigan, Monograph No. 35, 1964.

Stigler, George J. The Theory of Price, New York: The McMillan Co., 3rd edition, 1966.

Survey Research Center. "Housing", Statistical Report Number III, 1965, Survey of Consumer Finances, Economic Behavior Program.

Swift, William J., and Weisbrod, Burton A. "On the Monetary Value of Education's Intergeneration Effects", The Journal of Political Economy, Vol. LXXIII, No. 6, December, 1965.

Titmuss, Richard M. Income Distribution and Social Change, University of Toronto Press, 1962.

U.S. Bureau of the Census, Current Population Reports, Series P-60, No. 47, "Income in 1964 of Families and Persons in the United States", U.S. Government Printing Office, Washington, D.C., 1966.

_____, Income Distribution in the U.S., by Herman P. Miller, (A 1960 Census Monograph), U.S. Government Printing Office, Washington, D.C. 1966.

_____, Statistical Abstract of the United States: 1965. U.S. Government Printing Office, Washington, D.C. 1965, pp. 240-243.

_____, Statistical Abstract of the United States: 1966, U.S. Government Printing Office, Washington, D.C. 1966, Table No. 335.

U.S. Department of Commerce, Office of Business Economics, Survey
    of Current Business: April 1966, U.S. Government Printing
    Office, Washington, D.C. Vol. 46, No. 4, pp. 515-516.

U.S. Department of Commerce, Office of Business Economic, U.S.
    Income and Output: A supplement to the survey of current
    business, U.S. Government Printing Office, Washington,
    D.C., 1958, p.93.

Weisbrod, Burton R. "Education and Investment in Human Capital,"
    The Journal of Political Economy, Vol. LXX, No.5, part 2
    October, 1962, pp. 106-123.

Wharton, C.R. Jr. "Economic Meaning of Subsistence," The Malayan
    Economic Review, Vol. VIII, No.2, October 1963, pp. 46-58.

BIBLIOGRAPHY

Listed below are books and articles published or prepared in 1968 by the staff of the Economic Behavior Program of the Survey Research Center.

Barfield, Richard and James N. Morgan. *Early Retirement: The Decision and The Experience,* 1969.

Dunkelberg, William C. and Frank P. Stafford. The cost of financing automobile purchases. *Review of Economics and Statistics,* 1969.

Katona, George, James N. Morgan, and Richard E. Barfield. Retirement in prospect and retrospect. *Trends in Early Retirement* (Occasional Papers in Gerontology No. 4). Ann Arbor: The University of Michigan Institute of Gerontology, March 1969, 27-49.

Katona, George and Eva Mueller. *Consumer Response to Income Increases* (An Investigation Conducted in the Year of the Tax Cut). Washington, D.C.: Brookings Institution, 1968.

Katona, George. On the Function of Behavioral Theory and Behavioral Research in Economics. *American Economic Review,* LVIII, March 1968, 146-150.

Katona, George. Consumer Behavior: Theory and Findings on Expectations and Aspirations. Proceedings, *American Economic Review,* LVIII, 2, May 1968, 19-30.

Katona, George. Consumer Behavior and Monetary Policy. In *Geldtheorie und Geldpolitik* (Festschrift for Guenter Schmoelders). Berlin, Germany: Duncker and Humbolt, 1968, 117-132.

Lansing, John B., Charles Wade Clifton, and James N. Morgan. *New Homes and Poor People.* Ann Arbor: Institute for Social Research, 1969.

Morgan, James N. Family Use of Credit. *Journal of Home Economics, 60,* January 1968.

Morgan, James N. Some pilot studies of communication and consensus in the family. *Public Opinion Quarterly, 32,* 1, Spring 1968, 113-121.

Morgan, James N. The supply of effort, the measurement of well-being, and the dynamics of improvement. *American Economic Review, 58,* May 1968.

Morgan, James N. Survey analysis: applications in economics. In *International Encyclopedia of the Social Sciences, 15,* New York: Macmillan, 1968, 429-436.

Mueller, Eva. *Technological Advance in an Expanding Economy: Its Impact on a Cross-section of the Labor Force.* In press, to be released in September 1969.

Sonquist, John A. Problems of getting sociological data in and out of a computer. Paper read at the American Sociological Association, Boston, August 1968, 22 p.

Stafford, Frank P. Concentration and labor earnings: comment. *American Economic Review, 58,* 1, March 1968, 174-181.

Stafford, Frank P. Student family size in relation to current and expected income. *Journal of Political Economy,* 1969.

Data collected by the Economic Behavior Program are available on either punched cards or computer tapes, together with a detailed code describing the content of the cards or tapes. Thus, interested scholars or other parties may obtain or prepare further analysis beyond that presented in this volume.

SURVEY RESEARCH CENTER PUBLICATIONS

Survey Research Center publications should be ordered by author and title from the Publications Division, Department B, Institute for Social Research, The University of Michigan, P.O. Box 1248, Ann Arbor, Michigan 48106.

1960 Survey of Consumer Finances. 1961. $4 (paperbound), 310 pp.

1961 Survey of Consumer Finances. G. Katona, C. A. Lininger, J. N. Morgan, and E. Mueller. 1962. $4 (paperbound), $5 (cloth), 150 pp.

1962 Survey of Consumer Finances. G. Katona, C. A. Lininger, and R. F. Kosobud. 1963. $4 (paperbound), 310 pp.

1963 Survey of Consumer Finances. G. Katona, C. A. Lininger, and E. Mueller. 1964. $4 (paperbound), 262 pp.

1964 Survey of Consumer Finances. G. Katona, C. A. Lininger, and E. Mueller. 1965. $4 (paperbound), 245 pp.

1965 Survey of Consumer Finances. G. Katona, E. Mueller, J. Schmiedeskamp, and J. A. Sonquist. 1966. $4 (paperbound), $6 (cloth).

1966 Survey of Consumer Finances. G. Katona, E. Mueller, J. Schmiedeskamp, and J. A. Sonquist. 1967. $4 (paperbound), 303 pp.

1967 Survey of Consumer Finances. G. Katona, J. N. Morgan, J. Schmiedeskamp, and J. A. Sonquist. 1968. $5 (paperbound), $7 (cloth), 343 pp.

1968 Survey of Consumer Finances. G. Katona, W. C. Dunkelberg, J. Schmiedeskamp, and F. P. Stafford. 1969. $5 (paperbound), $7 (cloth), 287 pp.

Automobile Ownership and Residential Density. John B. Lansing and Gary Hendricks. 1967. $3, 230 pp.

The Geographical Mobility of Labor. John B. Lansing and Eva L. Mueller. 1967. $6.50, 421 pp.

Multiple Classification Analysis. James N. Morgan, John A. Sonquist and Frank M. Andrews. 1967. $3.

Productive Americans: A Study of How Individuals Contribute to Economic Progress. James N. Morgan, Ismail Sirageldin, and Nancy Baerwaldt. 1966. $5, 546 pp.

Residential Location and Urban Mobility: The Second Wave of Interviews. John B. Lansing. 1966. $2.50 (paperbound), 115 pp.

Private Pensions and Individual Saving. George Katona. 1965. $1.50 (paperbound), $2.50 (cloth), 114 pp.

Consumer Behavior of Individual Families Over Two and Three Years. Richard F. Kosobud and James N. Morgan (Editors). 1964. $5 (paperbound), $6 (cloth), 208 pp.

Residential Location and Urban Mobility. John B. Lansing and Eva Mueller. 1964. $2 (paperbound), 142 pp.

Residential Location and Urban Mobility: A Multivariate Analysis. John B. Lansing and Nancy Barth. 1964. $2 (paperbound), 98 pp.

The Travel Market, 1964-1965. John B. Lansing. 1965 $4 (cloth), 112 pp.

*The Changing Travel Market. John B. Lansing and Dwight M. Blood. 1964. $10 (cloth), 374 pp.

The Detection of Interaction Effects. John A. Sonquist and James N. Morgan. 1964. $3 (paperbound), 292 pp.

The Geographic Mobility of Labor, a First Report. John B. Lansing, Eva Mueller, William Ladd, and Nancy Barth. 1963. $3.95 (paperbound), 328 pp.

*The Travel Market 1958, 1959-1960, 1961-1962. John B. Lansing, Eva Mueller, and others. Reprinted 1963 (originally issued as three separate reports). $10, 388 pp.

*The Travel Market 1955, 1956, 1957. John B. Lansing and Ernest Lillienstein. Reprinted 1963 (originally issued as three separate reports). $10, 524 pp.

Location Decisions and Industrial Mobility in Michigan, 1961. Eva Mueller, Arnold Wilken, and Margaret Wood. 1962. $2.50 (paperbound), $3 (cloth), 115 pp.

*Package of three available for $25.00.

OTHER BOOKS BY MEMBERS OF
THE ECONOMIC BEHAVIOR PROGRAM

Transportation and Economic Policy. John B. Lansing. Free Press, 1966.

The Mass Consumption Society. George Katona. McGraw-Hill, 1964.

Income and Welfare in the United States. J. N. Morgan, M. H. David, W. J. Cohen, and H. E. Brazer. McGraw-Hill, 1962.

An Investigation of Response Error. J. B. Lansing, G. P. Ginsburg, and K. Braaten. Bureau of Economic and Business Research, University of Illinois, 1961.

The Powerful Consumer. George Katona. McGraw-Hill, 1960.

Business Looks at Banks: A Study of Business Behavior. G. Katona, S. Steinkamp, and A. Lauterbach. University of Michigan Press, 1957.

Consumer Economics. James N. Morgan. Prentice-Hall, 1955.

Contributions of Survey Methods to Economics. G. Katona, L. R. Klein, J. B. Lansing, and J. N. Morgan. Columbia University Press, 1957.

Psychological Analysis of Economic Behavior. George Katona. McGraw-Hill, 1951. (Paperback edition published in 1963.)

Economic Behavior of the Affluent. Robin Barlow, H. E. Brazer, and J. N. Morgan. Washington, D. C.: Brookings Institution, 1966.

Living Patterns and Attitudes in the Detroit Region. John B. Lansing and Gary Hendricks. A report for TALUS (Detroit Regional Transportation and Land Use Study), 1967, 241 pp. (Available only from TALUS, 1248 Washington Blvd., Detroit, Mich. 48226—$5 to nongovernmental agencies.)